7708

The Promise
of His Coming

A New Testament Study of the
Second Coming of Christ

By Stanley Horton

GOSPEL PUBLISHING HOUSE
Springfield, Missouri 65802

2-573

Contents

Preface

Is the second coming of Christ relevant to our lives today? In times of spiritual revival the return of Christ has always been a bright and living hope. But, too often, when the first wave of revival passes over, people settle down and the Second Coming seems far away. People ask what practical value does it have for us as we face our problems, as we try to fulfill our dreams.

It will help us then, to go through the New Testament and find out just what the Second Coming meant to those first Pentecostal believers who carried the gospel into a world that was in many ways different, but in surprisingly many ways like our own. The purpose of this book is to do just that. Starting with Old Testament prophecies and the four Gospels, the book considers the entire New Testament, except for the Book of Revelation. Revelation is worthy of a separate study. The King James version has been used except where the author has added additional meanings and insights from his study of the original Greek. Every attempt has been made to draw out the full picture of what Christ's coming and our blessed hope of glory really meant to the apostles and the Early Church. We live in the same age. We face the end of that age, and are far nearer to it than they. May God make the promise of His coming as real to us as it was to them.

May we as Sunday school and church workers apply to our lives and teaching the truth here discussed.

1 Seen From Afar

A STAR TO GUIDE

A famous teacher once said he did not need a star for he had a lamp in his hand. God's Word provides us with both. Touched and illuminated by the Spirit, the Word becomes a lamp to our feet and a light to our path.[1] The Word gives understanding, counsel, and guidance.[2] Compare the Word with the teachings of the heathen. See the morass of lies, half-truths, and immorality into which they fell. Their teachers presented conflicting philosophies and contradictory principles for life and action. Some taught that pleasure was the highest good. Some tried to ignore both pleasure and pain. Others used religion to justify sex orgies and drunkenness. In the ancient world God's Word presented the only consistent call to holiness and righteousness. No other book taught men what it really means to "do justly," that is, to show others the kind of love and mercy God shows us; and to "walk humbly" with the Lord.[3] We could have no better lamp. Mankind needs the teachings of God's holy Word.

A man who is lost needs more than a lamp to guide him, however. With nothing but a lamp in his hand he might still wander in circles getting nowhere. But let the stars come out and they will give him

---

[1] Psalm 119:105.
[2] Psalm 119:130, 133, 144.
[3] Micah 6:8.

5

direction. He will know where he is going. The
Bible points us to the star that gives life direction
and meaning. In a world that seems full of meaning-
lessness, it brings purpose, a goal, and a hope. It
is not only a holy Word, but a Word full of practical
wisdom, and it is the prophetic Word. God used many
men in ancient times. The key figures who laid the
foundations, taught the truth, and prepared the way
for the future were holy men, moved or borne along
by the Spirit of God—men known as prophets.[4]

We must not suppose that the prophets were concerned only with the future, however. Too often men
relegate prophecy to a time far away. They make it
seem unreal and unrelated to the problems of daily
life. As a matter of fact, only about five percent
of the messages of the prophets dealt with the distant future. Their primary concern was always the
needs of the people out in front of them, the people
to whom they ministered. Someone has said the prophets were first of all forthtellers and only secondarily
foretellers. The very word "prophet" was used to
mean a speaker or spokesman for God. God sent them
to declare His will to the people. Every one of them
made a powerful impact on their own day and time.
Every one of them brought God's answer to the
questions and problems of their own century. By
pointing to the future they did not turn their back on
the present. They did not discard the lamp in favor of
the star.

Does this mean that what they had to say about the
future was less important than what they had to say
about the present? Not at all. They used the prophecies of the future to give motive and incentive

[4] 2 Peter 1:21.

for obeying God's will in the present. The hope of the future reinforced and gave direction to the need and purpose to serve God. For example, Isaiah told the people of a time in the last days when God's house would be exalted and all nations would flow into it. People of many nations would say, "Come ye, and let us go up to the mountain of the Lord, to the house of the God of Jacob; and he will teach us of his ways, and we will walk in his paths,"[5] and then God would bring peace after judgment. But Isaiah did not tell them this just to satisfy their human curiosity about the future. He said all that in order to say this, "O house of Jacob, come ye, and let us walk in the light of the Lord."[6] In other words, some day men will come from everywhere seeking to learn and to follow the Lord. We have the light now. We have the opportunity to follow the Lord now. Why do we not do now what some day multitudes from all directions will want to do?

In another vein, Zephaniah tells of the Day of the Lord, "a day of wrath, a day of trouble and distress, a day of wasteness and desolation, a day of darkness and gloominess, a day of clouds and thick darkness,"[7] and a day of the fierce anger of the Lord.[8] Then he cries out to the people of his own day as well as to us, "Seek ye the Lord, all ye meek of the earth, which have wrought his judgment [justice]; seek righteousness, seek meekness: it may be ye shall be hid in the day of the Lord's anger."[9] Future judgment was thus used to provide an incentive for right attitudes in the present.

---

[5] Isaiah 2:3.
[6] Isaiah 2:5.
[7] Zephaniah 1:15.

[8] Zephaniah 2:13.
[9] Zephaniah 2:3.

A Twofold Message

This twofold message of judgment and hope runs through the entire Old Testament. Even in the Garden of Eden we see it. Man's sin and that of the tempter called for judgment. But in the midst of the pronouncement of judgment, God gave the first promise of the gospel: "I will put enmity between thee [the old serpent, Revelation 12:9] and the woman, and between thy seed [those who are of their father, the devil, John 8:44] and her seed [Christ, the one true seed, Galatians 3:16]; it [note the singular] shall bruise [crush] thy head, and thou shalt bruise his heel."[10] That is, Satan would try his best against Christ, but would not be able to hold Him, just as a wrestler cannot keep holding on to a man when all he is able to grasp is the heel. Christ's victory, however, would be complete and would totally crush the power of Satan.

How much of this did Adam and Eve understand? One of the principles of Scripture is that God gave the revelation of His will and plan in a step-by-step manner as men were prepared to receive it. But Adam and Eve understood enough to put their faith in the promise. It was at this time that Adam gave his wife the name Eve, "Life," indicating confidence in the hope that the serpent would be crushed and that the promised Seed would live. It indicated also the hope that all who placed their faith in God's promise would find spiritual life. Then, in response to Adam and Eve's newfound faith, God gave them a token of redemption by providing them with a coat of skins and thus indicating He had covered their sins.

Eve further expressed her faith and hope when she

---

[10] Genesis 3:15.

named her first son Cain, "one gotten" with the help
of the Lord. As Cain grew she was disappointed in
him, but not in the Lord. Because she kept her faith
in God and His promise she continued to live in touch
with the Lord. Other sons and daughters were born.
Among them was one whom she named Seth, "appointed one," because God gave her the assurance that
though this son was not the promised Seed, through
him the promised One would come.[11]

PROGRESSIVE REVELATION

As time went on, God continued this step-by-step
revelation. By this we do not mean that God gave the
people half-truths or anything that was a mixture
of truth and error. Sometimes in school children
learn an oversimplified explanation that they have to
unlearn later on. But this was nothing like God's
dealing. Everything He revealed was pure truth. But
He gave a little here and a little there, gradually
unfolding His will and plan.[12] Part of the reason for
this was because Jesus would have to come and bring
the fullness of the revelation in His own Person before
men could truly understand.

God, therefore, in preparation for what was to come,
gave a glimpse of the future here, and another glimpse
there. God's prophets, however, were quite different
from the heathen prophets, soothsayers, and prog-
nosticators. The heathen were concerned about what
would happen next. They looked for some way to
flatter the kings who employed them. But the true
prophets gave God's message regardless of who was
pleased and who was not. And, in most cases, God did
not give any clear indication of the times or seasons

---

[11] Genesis 4:25. [12] Hebrews 1:1.

or of what would happen next. Enoch caught a glimpse of the second coming of the Lord coming "with ten thousands of his saints."[13] Abraham, when he offered Isaac on Mount Moriah, caught a glimpse of how God would see man's need and provide a Substitute.[14] Moses promised a Prophet to come who would truly speak all God would command.[15] Unfortunately, the people of Israel did not always follow the Lord, and the prophets had to continue the twofold message of warning and of hope, with greater and greater emphasis on the judgment to come. The hope of God's promises, however, continued to be the great motivating force which kept many on the right road.

As the prophets continued to deal with the people, their messages concerning the future seemed to fall into four main categories: the Day of the Lord, the remnant that repents and returns, the coming King, and the coming Kingdom.

THE DAY OF THE LORD

The first promise in Genesis 3:15 pointed to the time when the head of the serpent, Satan, would be crushed. But that day could not come before the coming of the promised Seed. To prepare the way, God chose a man, Abraham, and a people, Israel. To Abraham He gave promises of a land and blessing. He promised also to bless those who blessed him and curse those who cursed him.[16]

A partial fulfillment of this came when God brought Israel from Egypt into the promised land. Plagues fell upon the pharaoh who opposed Israel, and God brought Israel out with a mighty hand. Then, at Sinai God brought Israel into covenant

---

[13] Jude 14.
[14] Genesis 22:8, 13, 14.
[15] Deuteronomy 18:15-19.
[16] Genesis 12:1-3.

relation with Himself as a chosen people. Upon the
condition of continuing to obey His voice and keep
His covenant, they would be a *peculiar* (valued,
choice, chosen, special) treasure to God, a kingdom
of priests, or, as the New Testament puts it, a royal
priesthood,[17] and a holy (dedicated, consecrated,
separated) nation.[18]

Further fulfillment of blessing came with Samuel,
David, and Solomon. The kingdom was established,
enemies defeated, and prosperity came beyond anything they had ever dreamed. But Samuel was not
able to prevent the self-will of Saul. David sinned.
Solomon fell into idolatry. Then, the nation was
divided into warring factions. Jeroboam set up golden
calves in Bethel and Dan, and many of the kings
turned away from the Lord. It was obvious that the
promises had not yet found their final fulfillment.

Though the Israelites fell into increasing sin and
worldliness, and though they often worshipped Baal
along with the Lord, they never forgot they were the
chosen people. In fact, they began to emphasize it
even more. They dreamed of the great day when the
Lord would overthrow all their enemies and crown
them with wisdom and honor. They multiplied their
sacrifices to the Lord and became more and more
diligent about keeping the forms of religion.

This became worse as the teachers of the people fell
into sin, and as false prophets arose who taught lies.[19]
Priests, who ought to have taught the people the
spiritual meaning of their worship, ceased teaching or
taught only what they were paid to teach.[20] The true
prophets whom God raised up were faithful to give

[17] 1 Peter 2:9.
[18] Exodus 19:4-6.
[19] Isaiah 43:27; 9:15.
[20] 2 Chronicles 15:3; Micah 3:11.

God's teaching, but the people as a whole refused instruction. They put on superior airs and mocked the prophets. The result was that the majority of the people no longer knew God in any real way. God had to say, "My people are destroyed for lack of knowledge: because thou hast rejected knowledge, I will also reject thee."[21]

To a luxury-loving, selfish people who talked a great deal about the coming day of the Lord, Amos had to say, "Woe unto you that desire the day of the Lord! to what end is it for you?"[22] For them, chosen people or not, the day of the Lord would be dark and terrible. Isaiah adds that the proud would then be brought low. They would try to hide in the rocks and in the dust.[23]

The prophets all give a black picture of this coming day, the Day of Judgment, the day of God's indignation. In it the Son will be revealed as Judge. He will break the nations, that is, all Christ-rejecting people, with a rod of iron as a shepherd breaks the bones of the enemies of the sheep.[24] He will tread the winepress of God's wrath alone.[25] "And the slain of the Lord shall be many."[26]

God's purpose was not to discourage the people, however. He wanted the prophets to teach the people these things so they could be warned and escape the wrath to come. Surely, in the midst of the sin, corruption, lust, and false philosophies which fill the world today, we need Sunday school teachers who will present the whole truth. Men need to know what to expect as God's plan unfolds. They need to know what

---

[21] Hosea 4:6.
[22] Amos 5:18.
[23] Isaiah 2:10-12.

[24] Psalm 2:9.
[25] Isaiah 63:3.
[26] Isaiah 66:16.

His requirements are with respect to righteousness, holiness, justice, mercy, and love.

THE REMNANT

God's purpose in judging Israel and the nations was not to destroy the people. God would always have a remnant. There would always be those who would love and serve Him. The first prophecies concerning the remnant were, however, not so much promises as threats. Amos compared Israel to a sheep captured by a lion where all that could be rescued were two legs or a piece of an ear—not much of a remnant.[27] In a time when false prophets were saying God's people could live as they pleased and He would never let anything happen to them, Isaiah indicated that only a tenth would return.[28] Yet, Amos did see that the godly would not be lost, and Jeremiah saw that God still had a place for the remnant of Israel in His plan.[29]

This teaching concerning the remnant received its fullest treatment in the Book of Isaiah in connection with what is said about the servant of the Lord. In Isaiah, the servant means the one who serves by getting his master's work done. The servant of the Lord is therefore the one who does the work of the Lord.

The phrase is used in different ways. Sometimes Isaiah uses it of the nation of Israel as a whole. They were called and chosen by God to carry out His will and do His work. The nation as a whole, as we have seen, failed. But within the nation was a godly remnant. In Elijah's day when he thought he was the only one left serving God, there was still a remnant of seven thousand who had not bowed the knee to

[27] Amos 3:12.
[28] Isaiah 6:13.
[29] Amos 9:8, 9; Jeremiah 30:11; 31:5-7.

Baal.[30] There was still a remnant in Isaiah's time,
and when Manasseh reintroduced idolatry into Jerusalem he had to fill Jerusalem from end to end with
the blood of the martyrs in order to do it.[31] God
has always had a witness in every age. But even this
godly remnant fell short. They were not free from
sin. They were unable to truly do the work of God.

Who, then, would do the work of God? Isaiah saw
coming from this godly remnant and from the seed of
David, One who would be the Servant of the Lord. He
would not fail. He would actually do God's work. The
climax is given in Isaiah 53. Other servant passages
include Isaiah 42:1-7; 49:1-6; 50:4-9; 61:1-3. Here we
see the Messiah or anointed Servant, not only suffering as our substitute, but as a result, triumphing,
coming as a Conqueror.[32]

THE COMING KING

The triumph of the Coming One is seen more clearly in passages which deal with Him as the coming
King. The hope of His triumph begins with the
promise of Genesis 3:15, the Seed of the woman.
Gradually, this is narrowed down to the seed of Seth,
of Noah, of Shem, of Abraham, of Isaac, of Jacob,
of Judah, and finally, of David. To David, God gave
a covenant guaranteeing that his line and throne
would be made eternal.[33] Individuals in David's line
would have to be punished if they sinned. But God
would always have a man for the throne.

David's own sons all failed, even Solomon. But
David caught a glimpse of a great Son, the Son of
God to whom God would give the heathen for His
inheritance and the uttermost part of the earth for

[30] 1 Kings 19:18.   [32] Isaiah 53:12.
[31] 2 Kings 21:16.   [33] 2 Samuel 7:12-16.

His possession, a Son to whom we must give our
homage and devotion, a Son who brings blessing when
we put our trust in Him.[34] This Son would make
David's throne eternal. Isaiah saw Him born of a
virgin and governing forever.[35] Daniel saw Him as
"one like the Son of man" coming in the clouds of
heaven and receiving dominion, glory, and a kingdom
that will never pass away.[36] Micah saw Him not only
as born in Bethlehem but as bringing peace and
victory.[37] Zechariah saw Him not only as the Priest
bringing cleansing, but as the Priest who would finish
His work and sit in glory on His throne.[38] Zechariah
also saw Him as the Lord who will come with "all
the saints" and when His feet touch the Mount of
Olives it will split down the middle leaving a great
valley.[39]

The Coming Kingdom

The promise of the coming of the King means also
the coming of His kingdom, for where the King is,
there is the kingdom. Daniel saw this future kingdom
filling the earth after the fall of the Babylon image
of Nebuchadnezzar's dream.[40] The curse will be lifted,
and the earth will know a new fertility.[41] Even the
deserts will blossom "like the garden of the Lord".[42]

More important, God will restore His people, give
them back their song and joy, give them peace and
wipe away their tears.[43] The prophets saw also that
this restoration would not be limited to Israel. God
wanted the Gentiles to share in it too. No longer will
a veil cover the eyes and hearts of the Gentiles, but

---

[34] Psalm 2:7, 8, 12.
[35] Isaiah 7:14; 9:6, 7; 11:10.
[36] Daniel 7:13, 14.
[37] Micah 5:2-5.
[38] Zechariah 3:4; 6:12, 13.
[39] Zechariah 14:4, 5.
[40] Daniel 2:34, 35, 44.
[41] Joel 3:18.
[42] Isaiah 51:3; 35:1.
[43] Isaiah 12:1-6; 25:8; 66:12.

they will say, "This is our God," and "many nations
will be joined to the Lord."[44] Gentiles and Jews
will share in a new ministry, and there will be an
inheritance for both even in the promised land.[45]
It will be truly evident then that the middle wall of
partition has been broken down and Christ has made
of the Jew and Gentile one new man.[46] And, since
the restoration of Israel will be on the basis of the
new covenant or testament, both Jews and Gentiles
will join in perfect worship and in the blessings of the
Spirit.[47]

The Old Testament prophets did not see the fullness of all that God has prepared. They sometimes
jump from the first coming to the second coming of
Christ and back again almost in the same breath, for
they did not see the time interval in between. But they
did see that the Lord will be King over all the
earth.[48] They did not see the interval of the Millennium either, for this was not revealed until John was
exiled to the Island of Patmos. But they saw that
beyond the restoration of this earth was a new heaven
and a new earth.[49] Then they took what God let
them see and taught the people to live so that they
would be ready. Sometimes it seemed that not many
were responding to the message. But they kept on
faithfully teaching, warning, and urging the people to
seek the Lord. They did it with a love in their heart
for God's people. And they often did it at the risk of
their lives. The New Testament makes them our
examples.

[44] Isaiah 25:9; Zechariah 2:11.
[45] Isaiah 62:10-12; 66:18;
    Ezekiel 47:21-23.
[46] Ephesians 2:14, 15.
[47] Jeremiah 31:31-34.
[48] Zechariah 14:9.
[49] Isaiah 65:17.

QUESTIONS

1. How much of the preaching of the prophets was concerned with the future? How did they make these future prophecies apply to their own day?

2. Why did God reveal the future in a step-by-step process?

3. What is meant by the "Day of the Lord" and what did the prophets emphasize concerning it?

4. How and why did so many of the teachers of Israel fail?

5. What did the prophets mean by a remnant? How is this related to Isaiah's teaching concerning the Servant of the Lord?

6. What is God's purpose in bringing back the King and restoring the Kingdom?

2 The Day Will Come

THE PROPHESIED KING

As we turn to the New Testament we see that at the time Jesus was born some were ready to receive Him into their hearts. Shepherds responded to the message and song of the angels. Though Zacharias, the father of John the Baptist, was at first filled with doubt, both he and Elisabeth his wife soon responded to the Spirit and gloried, not merely in their son, but in the Messiah he would declare.[1] Simeon, in the temple, was moved by the Holy Spirit to take the baby Jesus in his arms and thank God for Him.[2] The aged Anna not only gave thanks to the Lord, but spread the good news to others who looked for the promised redemption.[3]

Why were these people prepared? Though there had not been a writing prophet during the over four hundred years since Malachi, there were many faithful teachers. Ezra set them an example when he "prepared his heart to seek the law [teaching, instruction] of the Lord, and to do it, and to teach in Israel statutes and judgments [divine decisions]."[4] The fact that Anna is called a prophetess and that Simeon was prepared and used by the Holy Spirit shows they had not forgotten that God's work is done, not by human might or the power of human armies, but "by my spirit, saith the Lord."[5] Teachers who had the touch of the Spirit prepared these hearts for the first coming of Jesus. Sunday

---

[1] Luke 1:17, 41-45, 67-69, 76-78.
[2] Luke 2:25-35.
[3] Luke 2:38.
[4] Ezra 7:10.
[5] Zechariah 4:6.

18

school teachers who are filled with the Spirit are needed to prepare hearts for His second coming.

Those teachers just before the time of Christ did not have an easy time. Circumstances, world conditions gave no hint that His coming was near. Over 150 years before the Wise Men came, Israel did see a remarkable series of fulfilled prophecies that led up to the appearance of Antiochus Epiphanes, the little horn of Daniel 8:9, 23, a type of the Antichrist. The First Book of Maccabees[6] tells the thrilling story of how an aged priest, Mattathias, of the Hasmonean family became outraged when Antiochus set up an idol in the temple and sacrificed a pig on the altar. He and his sons led the faithful in a guerrilla warfare which finally drove out the intruder and enabled the Jews to purify the temple, restore the daily sacrifice, and make a great celebration which the Jews still memorialize in their feast of Hanukkah.

What followed was disappointing. The rest of the prophecies of Daniel were delayed. The deliverance from Antiochus was only a token of what God could do. The Hasmonean family ruled for a time, but eventually, the country fell into dissension between Pharisees and Sadducees and into civil war. The Romans saw their opportunity and intervened. Then, Herod, by clever political maneuvering, gained the throne, and from 37 B.C. this Idumean or Edomite ruled in Jerusalem. Murder and assassination marked his reign. He built theaters and heathen temples in Samaria and Caesarea, besides erecting palaces and places of entertainment in various parts of the land. Though he tried to appease the Jews by rebuilding

---

[6] An apocryphal book from the period between the Testaments. It is good history, though not inspired.

and adorning the temple in Jerusalem, the fulfillment of Old Testament prophecy must have seemed far away.

Herod and the priests and scribes (official teachers of the Scriptures) wanted to keep it that way. They were disturbed when the Wise Men came with news of One born King of the Jews. But the common folk who heard it were stirred to a new hope, a hope that looked to the second coming of Christ as well as the first, though they saw, not two comings, but only that God would fulfill His promise of both a Saviour and King.[7]

THE UNRECOGNIZED KING

When, after another thirty years, Jesus came preaching and teaching, the mass of the people of Israel did not recognize Him for who He really was. There were two chief reasons for this. One was that teachers of the day did not see the prophecies of the Old Testament in their proper perspective. In spite of Isaiah 53, Zechariah 6, and other prophecies, they did not understand that the Messiah had a twofold ministry as priest and king. They did not see that the priestly ministry had to come first, that the cross had to come before the crown. Because the days were dark and the Romans hated these teachers, they picked out the promises that seemed most appealing and ignored the rest. They taught a Messiah partly from the Scriptures and partly from their own imaginations, a Messiah who would be a political figure, overthrowing the Romans and setting the Jews on top of the world. Jesus was not their kind of Messiah.

The second reason why they failed to recognize Jesus was even more basic. The religious leaders did not know God in a personal way. The majority of the

---

[7] Luke 1:47, 69, 77; 2:30, 32.

people were out of touch with Him also. Jesus said of them, "Ye neither know me, nor my Father," and, "If God were your Father, ye would love me."[8]

In many cases this ignorance was willful. They "loved darkness rather than light, because their deeds were evil."[9] But even those who came to Jesus, even His closest followers had wrong teaching so ingrained into them that it was hard for them to understand spiritual things. It was hard to see God's plan. Nicodemus, a teacher of the Jews, had no understanding of the Spirit or of God's plan. The disciples wanted place and position. The teaching they had received had not prepared them to recognize Jesus for who and what He really is. When Peter finally made his great confession, "Thou art the Christ, the Son of the living God," Jesus replied, "Flesh and blood hath not revealed it unto thee, but my Father which is in heaven."[10]

From this we may see that wrong teaching will hinder men from preparing for Christ's coming and sin and unbelief will hinder them even more. Today, Sunday school teachers who have turned their backs on the world and sin and who know God and His Word are needed to prepare men for Christ to come again.

THE REJECTED KING

Because Jesus was not their kind of Messiah and because He refused to be their king when they tried to take Him and make Him king by force, the crowds rejected Jesus and turned their backs on Him. The jealous Jewish leaders hated Him and finally crucified Him. But the cross was not the end, though important

---

[8] John 8:19, 42.
[9] John 3:19.
[10] Matthew 16:16, 17.

and necessary. John the Baptist introduced Jesus as the Lamb of God. Jesus gave Himself willingly in our stead. But on this side of the cross stands the Resurrection and Ascension. Jesus now waits for that next step when the Father will send Him forth again and make His enemies His footstool.[11]

THE UNEXPECTED KING

Even after the Resurrection many who believed on Jesus were still filled with hopes that He would establish an earthly kingdom at that time. Jesus did not discourage their hope in the future kingdom, but He did have to point out that the times and the seasons are in God's hands, subject to His authority. Their business was not to worry about the time of His coming. Rather, it was to be His witnesses.[12]

This was not the first time Jesus dealt with the times and seasons. He knew what a test to a person's faith delay can be. Again and again He gave teaching to try to prepare His disciples for the long delay of His second coming, a delay that would cause many to come to the place where they no longer expected His coming.

John the Baptist was among the first to question about the times and seasons. At the Jordan River John called Jesus the Lamb of God who would take away the sin of the world.[13] But John put even greater emphasis on the work of judgment which Jesus must some day do. Jesus would be like a man cleaning out a threshing floor, gathering up the wheat and burning the chaff.[14] It is true that God has committed His work of judgment to Jesus.[15] But John did not see the

---

11 Hebrews 10:12, 13; Acts 2:35.   14 Matthew 3:10, 12.
12 Acts 1:6-8.   15 John 5:22, 27.
13 John 1:29.

time gap. He did not realize that God sent Jesus first, not to condemn the world, but to save it.[16] It would be a long time before Jesus would come in judgment. John, however, was not prepared to understand this. Like the others who looked to Jesus in that day, he hoped Jesus would bring the judgment at once. He probably supposed that Jesus would use the judgment to prepare the way for the promised salvation.

After Herod threw John in prison, John began to wonder. Why did Jesus not deliver him? Why did Jesus not bring judgment on Herod and those like him? John heard Jesus was doing many miracles. But so did Elijah and Elisha long before. Perhaps Jesus was just another prophet like them. Perhaps Jesus was just another forerunner like himself. Perhaps God's time had not yet come.

John had to know. He sent disciples to Jesus with the straightforward question, "Art thou he that should come, or do we look for another?"[17] Jesus let them watch for a while. Then He sent them back to tell John what they had seen and heard. "The blind see, the lame walk, the lepers are cleansed, the deaf hear, the dead are raised, to the poor the gospel is preached."[18] Jesus truly was doing God's work. He would continue to do God's work. John must not let the delay cause him to be offended or led astray. That is, he must not doubt that Jesus is the One.

Jesus' own followers and disciples had no such doubts at this time. Even when the crowds turned away and the Jewish leaders threatened Jesus, the disciples stuck with Him. They believed in Him. They saw He had the words of eternal life.[19] Yet, when

---

[16] John 3:17.
[17] Matthew 11:3.
[18] Luke 7:22.
[19] John 6:68.

Jesus tried to warn them of His sufferings and death, the words did not seem to convince them. Again and again He tried to prepare them for the cross and the delay that would follow, but the truth did not penetrate. When the time finally came for Jesus to go up to Jerusalem to die, He warned them once more in Matthew 20:19. The only result was that James and John had their mother come to Jesus asking Him to give them the places of honor on His left and right when He came into His kingdom.[20] This request stirred the other disciples to indignation. They also hoped that Jesus would soon come into His kingdom and give them places of honor. They felt they deserved the best places just as much as James and John.

Jesus dealt with them in two ways. He did not want His followers to be like the rulers of this world who play the tyrant and lord it over the unfortunate. Instead, they were to serve. Jesus Himself was their example. He came, not to be served or waited on, but to serve and to give His life.[21] Then Jesus gave them a parable to show them they were wrong in thinking that the kingdom of God would immediately appear.[22]

In this parable Jesus compared Himself to a certain nobleman who went into a far country to receive a kingdom and to return. Clearly, Jesus would not set up His kingdom at once. Later, the disciples understood that Jesus meant He must ascend to heaven and be enthroned there before He could return as King. The comparison to a journey to a far country also emphasizes that He would be gone a long time.

Just how long He would be gone, Jesus did not say.

---

[20] Matthew 20:20, 21.
[21] Matthew 20:25-28.

[22] Luke 19:11-27.

He would return in power and great glory. But the time of His return no man knows, not even the angels. The Father in heaven alone knows the day and the hour.[23]

God seems to have withheld this information in order to minimize the dangers of delay. If a man receives advance information of the exact time a thief is planning to break into his house, he will be ready and waiting.[24] If God had given in prophecy the exact date of Christ's coming, there would be a great flurry of preparation at that time. But what would happen while He was gone? There would be some good servants who would do the work the Lord had left them to do. But many would be tempted to follow the example of the bad servant who "shall say in his heart, My lord delayeth his coming; and shall begin to smite his fellowservants and to eat and drink with the drunken."[25] It is better that we do not know the time of Christ's coming. God wants us to do His work. We are more likely to be faithful if we know we must always be awake, ready at any time for His coming.[26]

Human nature seems to want to speculate about the future. From time to time men have set dates, named places, or waited on rooftops, mountains, or in caves. But the plain teaching of Jesus is that His coming will be both sudden and unexpected. Christians will not be taken by surprise because they will be waiting, ready for action, their lights burning, no matter how long the Lord's coming is delayed. Jesus compares them to servants who wait through the night for their master to return, ready at any moment to respond to

[23] Matthew 24:30, 36.
[24] Matthew 24:43.
[25] Matthew 24:48, 49.
[26] Matthew 24:42, 44, 50.

'his knock. They will be rewarded, not only by his return, but by a banquet in their honor.[27]

The Christian, too, will be warned by signs of Christ's coming. Christ's coming will be preceded by wars, earthquakes, famines, epidemics, "fearful sights and great signs" from heaven, "signs in the sun, and in the moon, and in the stars: and upon the earth distress of nations, with perplexity; the sea and the waves roaring; men's hearts failing them for fear."[28] But the Christian will only see these things begin to come to pass. He will not need to give his attention to the signs. Instead, he can look up, realizing His redemption or salvation is near.[29]

The Christian can only be taken by surprise if he lets himself become overcharged (burdened down) with surfeiting (carousing or dissipation), drunkenness, and the cares or worries and anxieties of everyday life.[30] But, even in spite of the signs, the world as a whole will be taken by surprise. They will be like someone who blunders into a trap or a snare. Jesus compares them to the world of Noah's day. In spite of the warnings, the preaching, the building of the ark, and the gathering of the animals, the people were unheeding and unprepared. They did not really believe anything would happen. The day the flood came dawned as any other day to them. They had their meals planned, their good times planned, their parties and weddings planned. But that day brought an end to the world as they knew it. In just the same way the world will go blindly on, making its own plans. But one day Jesus will come.

The important thing, then, is to be ready when

---

[27] Luke 12:35-38.
[28] Luke 21:11, 25, 26.

[29] Luke 21:31.
[30] Luke 21:34.

Jesus comes, no matter how long the delay. This calls for preparation, work, and endurance. In the parable of the ten virgins, the delay was so long that even the five wise virgins began to nod and finally fell asleep. But they had made preparation. They had inner spiritual resources. They were ready when suddenly they realized the bridegroom had come. The five foolish virgins found that it was too late then to prepare.[31] Jesus has gone to prepare a place for us but unless we prepare, we can have no part in it.[32]

The parable of the virgins does not tell the whole story, however. There is a sense in which we rest in the Lord, waiting for His coming. But it would be a serious mistake to suppose that we can sit around doing nothing and be ready. The happy servant, Jesus said, is the one who is found busy doing his master's work when his master breaks in on him.[33] In both the parables of the talents and the pounds Jesus pictured servants left behind to take care of their master's business. To them he said, "Occupy till I come."[34] "Occupy" does not mean occupy a seat or a couch. The word comes from the same root as "occupation," and means to do business. They were to take the money their master put in their hands and use it in some sort of business undertaking. The servants who did this were rewarded, whether they actually gained much or little. The only one condemned was the servant who did not want to be bothered and who hid the money, disobeying his master's command.

Later on, Jesus made it clear just what business should occupy our attention. We must watch and pray. But He has given us authority and to every man

---

[31] Matthew 25:1-13.
[32] John 14:3.
[33] Matthew 24:46.
[34] Luke 19:13.

a work to do.[35] All of this centers around the Great Commission. The last words of Jesus to His disciples were that they should go into all the world to preach or proclaim the gospel, the good news of the forgiveness of sins.[36] They must first wait for the promise of the Father that would clothe them with power from heaven.[37] Then they must expect the same power to be manifest in the lives of those who would respond to the gospel in faith and obedience.[38] They must also teach and make disciples or learners anxious to know more about Jesus.[39] Jesus promised to be with them in this, and when they stepped out and began to spread the gospel, they found He was. He not only gave them the consciousness of His presence, He worked with them, "confirming the word with signs following."[40]

It is one thing to start out well, however, and it is quite another thing to continue in the same high faith. Jesus knew this. He knew that the long delay before His coming would mean many temptations, tests, and trials. He knew there would be many times when it would be easy for discouragement to take over. At one time, He asked the question, "When the Son of man cometh, shall he find faith on the earth?"[41] He warned in this connection that men "ought always to pray, and not to faint" or become tired, discouraged, or despairing.[42] His followers would often have good reason for discouragement, especially when their own loved ones betrayed them and when they realized how the whole world hated them because of Jesus. "But," Jesus said, "he that shall endure unto the end, the

---

[35] Mark 13:33, 34.
[36] Mark 16:15; Luke 24:47.
[37] Luke 24:49.
[38] Mark 16:17, 18.

[39] Matthew 28:19, 20.
[40] Mark 16:20.
[41] Luke 18:8.
[42] Luke 18:1.

same shall be saved."[43] Endurance implies standing your ground when others flee, holding out when others give up, persevering and continuing steadfast and true no matter what others do.

This we can do if we remember three things. Jesus prayed for us.[44] Jesus went to the cross for us that we might have forgiveness, life, and victory. Jesus did all this that we might never have to be afraid and that we might realize that it is our "father's good pleasure" to give us the Kingdom.[45] In fact, if we remember these things, the delay will be good for us. It has given us opportunity to receive another Comforter, another Helper, the wonderful Holy Spirit.[46] He illuminates God's Word and guides us into all truth. He makes us His agents to convince and convict the world of sin, and of righteousness, and of judgment to come. He shows us things to come.[47] Above all, He makes Jesus real to us now, so that our love for Him, like Jacob's love for Rachel, will make the delay seem as nothing.

---

[43] Mark 13:13.   [45] Luke 12:32.   [47] John 16:8-13.
[44] John 17:9, 11, 20.   [46] John 16:7.

Questions

1. Was the first coming of Christ expected by the religious and political leaders of the day? Does this parallel our own day?

2. What were the chief reasons for so many not recognizing Jesus when He came the first time? What effect should this have on our lives today?

3. Why was it difficult for Jesus to prepare His disciples for the delay in establishing His kingdom on earth? Could the same attitude keep us from being prepared for His second coming?

4. Why is it a mistake to speculate about the time of Christ's coming?

5. How did Jesus illustrate that we should prepare for His coming?

6. What can keep us from fear and give us joy as we face the prospect of Christ's coming?

3 A Necessary Consummation

AN END IN VIEW

Where did we come from? Where are we going? These are questions which often engage the minds of thinking men and women. The Old Testament gives us a simple but clear answer. In the beginning God created the heavens and the earth. In the end He will create a new heaven and a new earth. The New Testament gives us additional details of God's plan.

Mankind as a whole has ignored the plan of God. Over the centuries scientists, philosophers, and common folk have speculated again and again about the past and the future. Theories come and go. One of the most popular theories in recent times is the "steady state theory." This theory claims that the universe had no beginning in time and that it will be maintained forever by continuous creation of new high energy material out of nothing.

This steady state theory suited the materialists who say there is no God, no beginning, and no end. But recent discoveries in connection with distant stars do not fit the theory. Neither does the new discovery of microwave radiation which reaches the earth from all directions. The evidence from astronomy shows that the universe as we know it did have a beginning —and if a beginning, why not an end?

Viewed from the standpoint of the natural mind, the prospect is not pleasant. If bombs do not destroy mankind, air pollution may. If man somehow solves these problems and even if he produces a race of supergeniuses, the sun may explode into a nova and envelop the habitable planets with "H" bomb heat. If he escapes that, the universe, according to the second law of thermodynamics, is running down. All this removes reasonable hope that man may ultimately solve all his problems on his own. Biology now lacks evidence of any consistent goal in nature. Uncertainty rules science and philosophy. No one is sure any more whether there is any such thing as progress. Most of the so-called primitive people in the world today are really remnants of former highly developed civilizations wrecked at their height by increasing greed and immorality. Modern trends parallel those which brought those former civilizations to an end. None of them believed the end would come. Most of them were so drunk with pleasure and success they failed to see it coming and refused all warnings. If present trends continue the end will come and those who survive the wreckage may be forced to live under Stone Age conditions.

Too often those who speak of Christ's second coming have been called pessimists. In view of what has just been said, those who leave God out are the real pessimists. Modern discoveries are seldom good news. World War I, the war to end wars, left the seeds for World War II. World War II left the seeds for the cold war and the present conflicts.

Actually, there is very little good news in the world apart from the gospel. The very meaning of the word gospel is good news, and it is the good news the world still most desperately needs. It is good news that God loved the world enough to send His Son to die for us. It is good news that we have forgiveness of sin, healing, and blessing through His shed blood. It is good news that God raised Jesus from the dead and through Him gives us sure and certain access to God and heaven as well as hope for the future.

An important part of the good news is that the end of this age need not be a tragedy. For those who place their faith in Christ it will be a climax, a consummation. When Jesus said, "Lo, I am with you alway, even unto the end of the world," the literal meaning of the Greek is "unto the consummation of the age."[1] This means that the end will not merely mean that the present age will be over. Everything will shape up to a divinely appointed consummation. God's plan will be carried out, and a new and better age will begin. Our God is able to make even the wrath of man praise Him.[2] He is able also to take the devious plans of man and overrule them all until they help fulfill His plan. We may not always be able to see in advance just how God will do this. But we can be sure He will. Though Jesus saw a long delay before His second coming, He always kept the coming consummation in view.

THE END IS NOT YET

A few days before Jesus went to the cross, His disciples asked, "What shall be the sign of thy coming, and of the end of the world?"[3] The word "coming" in Greek is *parousia*. It was a word commonly used for the visit of an emperor to one of his provinces. The disciples used it because they were thinking of Christ's coming in power and great glory. They connected it with the "end of the world," as in Matthew 28:20 which means the consummation of this present age.

[1] Matthew 28:20.   [3] Matthew 24:3.
[2] Psalm 76:10.

The question rose out of an uneasiness in the minds of the disciples. All during that day the Jewish leaders opposed Jesus and questioned His authority. Jesus, in turn, warned them that publicans and harlots would go into the Kingdom before them. They would be destroyed and the Lord's vineyard given to others to care for. Their city would be burned.[4] They would not be able to escape the judgment of hell or *gehenna* (the place of final, eternal punishment).[5] The stone which the builders rejected (that is, Jesus Himself) would become the head of the corner.[6] But Jerusalem's house (the temple) would be abandoned.[7] This disturbed the disciples. How could this be? Surely, any calamity which would destroy the temple would bring the end of the age.

Jesus did not answer their question right away. He saw that too great a concern over the signs of the end could lead them astray, could keep them from doing the work God had for them to do. Strange and unusual events would mark the course of this age. False teachers would use them to try to draw a following after themselves. Jesus, therefore, took time to warn His disciples of distractions which might draw their attention away from the one great task of spreading the gospel.

Matthew 24:4-14 deals with these things which Jesus says are *not* signs of the end.

1. *Deceivers and false Christs.* The world will not see Jesus again until He comes in power and great glory.[8] From time to time people will say Christ is here or there, or out in the desert, or in some secret or hidden place.[9] But we are not to believe

---

[4] Matthew 21:31, 41; 22:7.
[5] Matthew 23:33.
[6] Matthew 21:42.
[7] Matthew 23:28.
[8] Matthew 24:30.
[9] Matthew 24:23, 26.

them. Neither are we to suppose that the rise of
one or even of a number of false Christs is a sign
of the end. There have been false Christs in every
period of the history of the Church. From time to
time there will be others. Let us not permit them
to distract us. Our best weapon against them is the
positive preaching of the truth of the gospel.

2. *Wars, rumors of wars, famine, pestilences, and
earthquakes.* These things must come from time to
time until Jesus returns to remove the curse from
the earth. Some still suppose that the purpose of
Christ's first coming was to bring peace to the world.
Jesus did promise His peace to His followers. But
He saw that the gospel would bring people face to
face with the necessity of making a decision. Some
would accept. Some would reject. The result would
be division cutting like a sword even through families.[10] A Christ-rejecting world would still be dominated by greed and selfishness. Wars would come,
and one war would lead to another. We must not
permit wars and calamities to trouble us, frighten us,
or disturb us in our purpose to spread the good news
that Jesus is victor.

Christian love will help us to meet the physical
and material needs of the victims of such calamities.
But it will not allow us to become so taken up with
social work that we forget that the spiritual need of
men is even greater. Wars, famines, pestilences, and
earthquakes are not signs of the end. They are only
opportunities for us to move in as ambassadors for
Christ.

3. *Persecution.* Persecution came quickly to the
Early Church and the apostles. But they did not

---
[10] Matthew 10:34-36; Luke 12:51-53.

give up and run. Filled with the Spirit, they dared to stand even before the same Jewish court that condemned Jesus. Instead of compromising, they bore powerful witness to the risen Christ. Persecution was never continuous, but it has come again and again through the history of the Church. In some countries Christians are suffering today. But we must not suppose simply because we find ourselves under terrible persecution that the end has come.

4. *Apostasy.* Persecutions will cause many to take offense, stumble, and fall into sin. The rise of false prophets who work miracles will deceive many and turn them from the simplicity of the gospel. The increase and spread of iniquity or lawlessness and godlessness will cause the fire of love for Christ to go out in many hearts and they will grow cold. Here again, this in itself is not a sign of the end. Church history has seen many times of coldness. During the Dark Ages in Europe it seemed that the light of the gospel almost went out. In America after the Revolutionary War, skepticism was rampant and it would have been hard to find a college student who was a witness for Christ. The true believer does not let the sin, false doctrine, and coldness around him distract him. He keeps on spreading the gospel, believing God for revival.

Matthew 24:13, 14 gives the positive side to the course of this age. All the negative things just mentioned warn us that we must stand our ground no matter what happens. But whoever endures or stands his ground to the end will be saved. Here, of course, the word "saved" means more than converted. Bible students recognize that there is a sense in which we have been saved, we are being saved, and we shall be saved. There is an ultimate salvation, a part of the final consummation of God's plan for us. We must not only take our stand for Christ if we would share in that; we must continue to stand our ground.

Jesus quickly connects this with the work of spreading the gospel as a witness to all nations. The best way to be sure we will stand our ground is to take an active part and to be a witness ourselves. Some Bible students do not feel that Matthew 24:14 applies to the course of this age. But even if this view is adopted, it does not excuse us from our responsibility in any way. Actually, this verse parallels the command to go and teach (make real students) of all nations, "and that repentance and remission [forgiveness] of sins should be preached in his name among all nations, beginning at Jerusalem."[11] It is good news that Christ is King. It is good news that His royal power demonstrated in His resurrection guarantees His final triumph and ours.

His kingly power also guarantees that the gospel will be preached, it must be preached. If we are faithful witnesses we shall share in the glory and the reward. If not, God will raise up others who will be faithful. God will have a people redeemed by the blood of Jesus "out of every kindred, and tongue, and people, and nation."[12] Until He gets them, the end will not come. We need, then, not more concern about what is going to happen next, but more concern over the spread of the gospel.

THE END—TRIBULATION

The time came when Jerusalem's enemies surrounded it, blockaded it, and leveled it to the ground, just as Jesus prophesied.[13] The Romans then rebuilt

---

[11] Luke 24:47.
[12] Revelation 5:9.

[13] Luke 19:43, 44.

it as a Gentile city. But it was not the end. Jerusalem was to be under Gentile domination until the "times of the Gentiles be fulfilled."[14] At the time of this writing the Gentiles still dominate the old city of Jerusalem. The end has not yet come. When it does come it will not bring peace and blessing, however. Instead, there will be for Jerusalem and the Jews days of great tribulation, greater than any yet known.[15] The Book of Revelation goes into more detail on this subject. It is not our purpose to do so here.

THE END—CHRIST'S RETURN

The fact that the world is headed for great tribulation refutes the common idea that the Kingdom must come in gradually. When the Pharisees asked Jesus when the kingdom of God would come, He told them that it would not come in such a way that its rise could be watched or observed. In this age God's rule or kingdom will be present only in men's hearts. But the time will come when Jesus will return. It will be a sudden event, like a lightning flash. Like the lightning also, we shall see it as we look up. Jesus compared it also to the sudden appearance of eagles or vultures when an animal dies in the desert. There may be nothing in sight for miles around, but suddenly, out of the sky, the vultures swoop down.[16]

As Jesus continues to deal with the events of His coming, He discusses two aspects. The first is in Matthew 24:29, 30. He describes a coming in power and great glory "after the tribulation of those days." This coming will be after great signs in the heavens, signs such as we find in Revelation 9 and 16. Luke adds that the time preceding this coming will include

---

[14] Luke 21:24.　　　　　　　　　　[16] Luke 17:20-24, 37.
[15] Matthew 24:21.

distress or anguish among the nations or Gentiles with
perplexity or anxiety because of the roaring of the
sea. (The sea may represent armies.) Men will be
fainting from fear and from the expectation of what
is coming on the inhabited earth.[17]

Second, in Matthew 24:31, Jesus goes back to the
gathering of true believers, a gathering which will
actually precede both the Great Tribulation and the
coming in power and great glory. The word "then" in
Matthew 24:30 is a very general word meaning "in
the same general period." Jesus, in dealing with His
coming, deals with a period of time which includes
both His coming for His elect or chosen (that is for
true believers and which also includes His coming in
glory) and a coming that the whole world will see.
But Jesus does not deal with this period in a chrono-
logical fashion. The Old Testament prophets jumped
from the first coming to the Second Coming without
indicating the time period between. So Jesus speaks
of one aspect of His coming and then another, not
always in order, and without indicating the time
interval in between. A comparison with other Scripture passages shows that the interval is there, however,
as we shall see later.

THE END—RESURRECTION

Another important event that will come in the end
of the age is the resurrection of all who have believed
in Christ and kept their trust in Him. The climax of
all four Gospels is the resurrection of Jesus. The
great significance of His resurrection is that it was
positive evidence that the Father accepted Christ's
sacrifice, so that through Christ we stand forgiven,

[17] Luke 21:25, 26.

cleansed, redeemed, justified. His resurrection also guarantees ours and assures us of the truth of the whole Christian revelation.

The Sadducees in New Testament times accepted the view of Greek materialism that the soul is just a function of the body. They denied immortality and therefore had no place in their thinking for a resurrection. When they questioned Jesus, He told them they did not really know the Scriptures nor did they know the power of God.[18] The majority of the Jews, however, did believe in a resurrection "at the last day."[19]

Jesus added to this that the condition for resurrection was belief in Him, for He is the source of resurrection and life.[20] In addition, "whosoever liveth," that is, whoever is resurrected and restored to life, "shall never die."[21] The raising of Lazarus was a testimony to Christ's life-giving power. Lazarus, however, came forth bound and had to be loosed. Lazarus, apparently, did die again. But Jesus rose right up through the graveclothes, leaving the wrappings, still intertwined, there in the empty tomb. Our resurrection will be like His. We shall be changed. As Jesus told the Sadducees, in the Resurrection we shall be as the angels, neither marrying nor given in marriage."[22]

Jesus also taught that He will be the one to summon the dead from their graves. He will do this in two separate resurrections. Those who have done good (literally, "the good," that is, the works of faith, hope, and love) come forth into a resurrection of life. Those who practiced evil or busied themselves with base or worthless things (worthless in God's eyes)

---

[18] Matthew 22:23-33.
[19] John 11:24.
[20] John 11:25.

[21] John 11:26.
[22] Mark 12:25.

come forth to a resurrection of damnation or judgment.[23] Some teach that these resurrections are simul-
taneous because of the word "hour." The word is
used, however, as John used it when he wrote, "It is
the last time."[24] It indicates a period of time. Revelation 20 finally gives the additional facts which show
that a thousand years separate these two resurrections.

The End—Rewards and Punishments

Jesus did not always distinguish between the two
resurrections as He did in John 5:29. His usual purpose was not to define the times and seasons or to
present the order of events. He was more interested
in presenting truths which would encourage us to live
so that we would be ready when He comes. In a
number of parables Jesus simply emphasizes the fact
of His coming along with the results of His coming.[25]
Sometimes He emphasizes judgment first, sometimes
rewards, depending on which He wants to give most
prominence in the lesson.

The chief thing which should concern us is that
there will be a harvest, a day of reckoning, a settling
of accounts.[26] Sinners will not escape. We cannot drift
along supposing that everything will turn out all right
no matter what we do. What we receive from the Lord
we have a responsibility to use for Him. The parable
of the talents, for example, shows that anyone who
uses what he has to do God's work will be rewarded
for his faithfulness. Those who turn their backs on
God's will and live self-centeredly, or even if they
just put off doing what they know they should do,
will lose everything. The Lord will call them un-

---

[23] John 5:28, 29.   [26] Matthew 12:38-42; 13:38, 39; 25:19.
[24] 1 John 2:18.
[25] The parable of the dragnet, Matthew 13:47-50, is an example.

profitable, worthless, miserable servants and will have them cast into outer darkness.[27]

The fact that Jesus will be the Judge is another truth which we must not overlook. Jesus said, "The Father judgeth no man, but hath committed all judgment unto the Son."[28] At the resurrection of the righteous, He will give out the rewards. At the resurrection of the wicked, He will pronounce the final judgments. This is brought out in Matthew 25:31-46. Some take this to be a judgment of living nations at the beginning of the Millennium. Others take it as a condensed or foreshortened picture which includes both the judgment seat of Christ before the Millennium and the great white throne judgment after the Millennium. The important thing is that those who do receive rewards, an inheritance, and a kingdom have not only received the grace and love of Christ, but have made themselves channels of that grace and love to others. Christ will have the preeminent position then. We must make Him preeminent in our lives and our churches now.

We make Him preeminent when we accept His message and put it into practice in our lives. Those who reject His message will be judged on the last day.[29] Those ashamed of Him and His teaching now will find Him ashamed of them when He comes in glory.[30] Though God is patient and longsuffering, if we do not obey Him, Jesus will send His holy angels in that day and He will reward or repay everyone according to his words or deeds.[31] "Watch ye therefore, and pray always, that ye may be accounted

[27] Matthew 25:14-30.
[28] John 5:22.
[29] John 12:48.
[30] Mark 8:38.
[31] Matthew 13:39, 41.

worthy to escape all these things that shall come to pass, and to stand before the Son of man."[32]

The End—the Kingdom

Though Jesus taught that Old Testament prophecies of the Kingdom would be postponed, He never denied that the Kingdom would come. He rather encouraged His followers to look forward to it. Very emphatically, He pointed out that the inheritance God has for us includes both eternal life and the Kingdom—a kingdom which God has prepared "from the foundation of the world."[33] Jesus must first suffer, but the prophesied glory would come in due time.[34]

The twelve apostles, Jesus said, would have a special place in the Kingdom, sitting on twelve thrones, judging the twelve tribes of Israel.[35] Jesus Himself will rule from the throne of His father David, fulfilling the prophecies of the Old Testament.[36] Then the Kingdom or rule of Heaven will come on earth, as Jesus taught us to pray that it would. Nor will the apostles be the only ones to share in the glory, for "Then shall the righteous shine forth as the sun in the kingdom of their Father."[37]

Jesus often compared this time to a wedding feast. Though many will reject the invitation, the command of the Lord is to go out where the people are and bring them in. He promises a measure of success, too, for "many shall come from the east and west, and shall sit down with Abraham, and Isaac, and Jacob, in the kingdom of heaven."[38] Jesus Himself looks forward to that time when He will drink the fruit of the vine

---

[32] Luke 21:36.
[33] Matthew 25:34, 46.
[34] Luke 24:26.
[35] Matthew 19:28.

[36] Luke 1:32, 33; John 7:42; Isaiah 9:6, 7.
[37] Matthew 13:43.
[38] Matthew 8:11.

with us in the kingdom of God.[39] Though we live in the last part of the age, we can share richly in this joy, for many of the last will be first, and many of the first last.[40] We have just as great an opportunity to be faithful as any of the saints and martyrs of past ages. It is the Father's good pleasure to give us the Kingdom. Do we consider the rewards valuable enough? Are we really waiting for Jesus to come?

---

[39] Luke 22:18, 29, 30.   [40] Matthew 19:30.

QUESTIONS

1. Why are those who hope for the Second Coming the true optimists?

2. What things did Jesus say are not signs of His coming?

3. Why is the coming of Christ delayed?

4. What are the two main aspects of Christ's coming? Does Jesus always indicate the time gap between?

5. What are the two great resurrections and their significance?

6. Locate other parables which emphasize that judgment will separate between the righteous and the wicked. (See Matthew 13:30, 48; 25:32.)

7. What did Jesus teach about the basis for the judgment of rewards and punishment?

8. What are some of the teachings of Jesus about the future Kingdom?

4 Pentecostal Preaching

THY KINGDOM COME!

What was the chief concern of the risen Christ? Was it the "many infallible proofs," by which He convinced the disciples of His resurrection? Was it the "promise of the Father" that His followers would be baptized in the Holy Ghost? These things were very important. They had to be convinced of the reality of His resurrection if they were to be witnesses of it. They had to be sure that He was no ghost, no mere spirit, but the same Jesus actually come back to life. Then they needed the power of the Holy Spirit to be able to take the good news to others.

Jesus did not have to stay on earth forty days after His resurrection to prove its reality, however. Nor did He have to stay forty days to give the promise of the coming of the Spirit. One thing kept Him from leaving any sooner. He saw that the disciples needed more teaching. He spent the forty days "speaking of the things pertaining to the kingdom of God."[1]

On the day He arose, He walked with two discouraged disciples on the road to Emmaus. They recognized that Jesus was a prophet. They had hoped that Jesus would redeem Israel. But they saw the death of Jesus as the end of their hopes. Jesus said to them, "O fools [unintelligent ones], and slow of heart [dull of understanding] to believe all that the

---

[1] Acts 1:3.

44

prophets have spoken: ought not Christ to have suffered these things, and to enter into his glory? And beginning at Moses and all the prophets, he expounded . . . the things concerning himself" until their hearts burned within them.[2]

Later the same day Jesus appeared to those gathered with the twelve in the Upper Room. After showing them His hands and feet and then eating a piece of broiled fish and a honeycomb, He said, "These are the words which I spake unto you, while I was yet with you, that all things must be fulfilled, which were written in the law of Moses, and in the prophets, and in the Psalms, concerning me. Then opened he their understanding that they might understand the scriptures."[3]

We see from this that the heart of what Jesus taught them about the Kingdom was "the things concerning Himself." Peter, on the Day of Pentecost, understood this. After explaining that the Pentecostal outpouring of the Spirit was in fulfillment of the prophecy of Joel, Peter went on to talk about the significance of Christ's death and resurrection. Immediately, he connected it with Psalm 16:10; "for thou wilt not leave my soul in hell [Greek, *Hades,* Hebrew, *Sheol;* the place of the departed spirits]; neither wilt thou suffer thine Holy One to see corruption [that is, in the grave]."[4] Peter first points out that this could not possibly apply to David. His tomb was right there in Jerusalem. His body did see corruption. Psalm 16:10 therefore prophesies that God, in faithfulness to His promise to David, would raise up a son of David, Christ, to sit on David's throne.[5]

---

[2] Luke 24:25-27, 32.
[3] Luke 24:44, 45.
[4] Acts 2:27.
[5] Acts 2:30.

Paul, preaching at Antioch in Pisidia on his first missionary journey, quoted the same psalm.[6] He quoted also the second psalm, "Thou art my Son, this day have I begotten thee."[7] This was a technical phrase. It had nothing to do with physical begetting. Rather, it was used as a special formula by kings when they wanted to elevate a son to the position and status of king, to reign as an equal on the throne. By the Resurrection and Ascension God exalted Jesus to the throne to share it with Him. (See Revelation 5:13 where blessing, honor, glory, and power are ascribed equally to the Father and to the Son.) David, therefore, in the second psalm was prophesying of the same thing Paul talks about in Philippians 2:9-11, "Wherefore [because Jesus humbled himself and went to the cross] God also hath highly exalted him, and given him a name which is above every name: That at the name of Jesus every knee should bow [that is, as to a king], of things in heaven, and things in earth, and things under the earth; And that every tongue should confess that Jesus Christ is Lord, to the glory of God the Father."

With this in mind we can see why Paul at Pisidian Antioch went on to connect the prophecy of Psalm 2:7 with God's promise to give "the sure mercies of David," that is, to be faithful to put a Son of David on the throne and to make that throne eternal. God did more than raise Jesus from the dead. He raised Him to the throne. Jesus will reign. Because He is King, there will be a kingdom.

The hardest thing for the disciples to understand about the Kingdom was still the time of its coming. In spite of all the parables and warnings, they could

---

[6] Acts 13:35.   [7] Psalm 2:7.

not seem to rid themselves of their old hopes for a worldly, political kingdom which would overthrow the Roman Empire. The cross brought those dreams to an end. But when Jesus rose, they soon had renewed visions of riding into power on the crest of a great wave of victory over the nations. Even after forty days of teaching, their uppermost thought was "Lord, wilt thou at this time restore again the kingdom to Israel?"[8]

Jesus did not give them the answer they wanted to hear. He had already told them that God alone knows the day and the hour. Now He emphasizes that it is not for them to know the times and seasons. They could afford to leave the future in God's hands. Jesus seems to imply also that the times and seasons are really none of their business. We cannot hurry God. Our speculations will not bring Christ back. It may, in fact, hinder us from doing God's work if we spend too much time trying to figure out what is going to happen next or just when Jesus will return.

That is why Jesus immediately focused the attention of His followers on God's real purpose for this age. The times and seasons were not their business. They were to be too busy being Christ's witnesses "in Jerusalem, and in all Judaea, and in Samaria, and unto the uttermost part of the earth."[9] The power of the Spirit would be given, not to reveal the distant future, but to get the gospel out. By telling them they were to be witnesses to the uttermost part of the earth, Jesus again indicated it would be some time before He returned. The Early Church at first hoped they would be able to spread the gospel to "the uttermost part" in the first generation. Many passages in the New

[8] Acts 1:6.   [9] Acts 1:8.

Testament reflect a hope that they would live to see Jesus return. But when they began to realize this would not be the case, they were not disappointed. They saw the greatness of the task. They saw how wonderful would be the reward. They gave their lives to spreading the gospel with a joy that did not depend on whether they would live to see Jesus return or not. He was with them. His Holy Spirit inspired and em- powered them. They knew He would keep His prom- ise and they would share in His kingdom whenever He comes.

THE MANNER OF HIS COMING

The apostles and those with them could never lose the vision of His coming. They had seen Him go. They could never forget how Jesus lifted His hands to bless them and then began to ascend into the heavens. Then, a cloud appeared, swept under Him, and lifted Him rapidly, and took Him out of their sight.

This cloud spoke of the glory into which Jesus ascended. A glory cloud often accompanied the mani- festation of God's presence in Old Testament times. One swept over the scene when Jesus was transfigured on the mountain in Galilee.[10] Glory clouds will there- fore mark the return of our Lord.[11] The disciples did not understand this at first. But two angels ap- peared and made it clear. Their words could hardly be more emphatic or more clear. "This same Jesus, which is taken up from you into heaven, shall so come in like manner as ye have seen him go into heaven."[12] His return would be just as literal and just as real as His ascension.

---

[10] Matthew 17:5.   [12] Acts 1:11.
[11] Matthew 24:30; 26:64.

The angels did more than assure the disciples of Christ's return, however. They asked the disciples why they still stood there staring into the heavens. They seemed to want to draw their attention back to the work Jesus had given them to do. They must wait in Jerusalem until they were clothed with power. Then they must go out with the gospel. Those who are truly waiting for Christ's coming do not keep their eyes focused on the skies, but on the harvest.

Nevertheless, the Ascension remained an important visible sign pointing to Christ's second coming. Jesus comes to us now in times of need and in times of refreshing.[13] But it is a tremendous encouragement to know that Jesus is also coming in glory and victory. On the Day of Pentecost, Peter reminded his hearers that "David is not ascended into the heavens: but he saith himself, The Lord said unto my Lord, Sit thou on my right hand, Until I make thy foes thy footstool."[14] Wicked men and the forces of Satan may seem to prevail for a time. But Jesus has already ascended to the Father's throne. He is already Victor, and God will bring about His final triumph.

CHRIST'S RESURRECTION AND OURS

Another thing kept the disciples from being disappointed when they faced death. Their hope was not simply in the Second Coming, but in the Resurrection. The heart of the good news, the gospel, was not simply salvation from sin, not merely forgiveness, not even the hope of heaven, important and wonderful as all these are. The very heart and center of the witness of all the Early Church was the resurrection of Christ. His resurrection took away the stigma of hanging, the shame of the cross. His resurrection demonstrated

---

[13] Acts 3:19.   [14] Acts 2:34, 35.

God's power and God's acceptance of Christ's sacrifice. His resurrection guarantees ours.

The hope of the Resurrection made the promises of Jesus real. Christ's prophecy that the twelve apostles would sit on twelve thrones judging the twelve tribes of Israel may have seemed vague and far away to the disciples when He first gave it. But after His resurrection it was made real to them. They had a *bishoprick* or overseership. Since Judas had chosen the wrong way and fulfilled Scripture by betraying Jesus, Judas lost out. The apostles then thought it only according to Scripture that another should be chosen to take the place of Judas. They also felt that Jesus had a purpose in choosing twelve as primary witnesses, so Peter, as their spokesman, said one must "be ordained to be a witness with us of his resurrection."[15]

The teaching and preaching of the resurrection of Jesus continued to be central in all the witness of the Early Church. On the Day of Pentecost, the apostles and those who were with them were all filled with the Holy Spirit, all spoke in tongues as the Spirit gave them utterance and told of the wonderful works of God.[16] Then Peter stood up with the twelve and began to speak. Here, the Greek word is "uttered forth." His words came from the Holy Spirit, not from himself. Notice that the recurring theme of this God-given, Spirit-inspired message is the Resurrection. Peter spoke of Jesus "Whom God hath raised up."[17]

Later, Peter drew attention to the significance of the Resurrection by calling Jesus the "Prince of life, whom God hath raised from the dead."[18] The word "prince" is not the ordinary word in the Greek. It

---

[15] Acts 1:22.
[16] Acts 2:1-4, 11.

[17] Acts 2:24, 32.
[18] Acts 3:15.

does mean a leader or a ruler. But it also means an originator, a founder. In Hebrews 2:10 it is translated "captain," and in Hebrews 12:2, "author." The Resurrection designated Jesus as the source, the founder, the author of life. Through Him we have life. Through Him we shall have resurrection.

When the gospel was taken to the Gentiles, the Resurrection had this same central place. At the house of Cornelius, Peter said of Jesus, "Him God raised up the third day, and shewed him openly."[19] Everywhere the Apostle Paul went, He proclaimed the Resurrection. At Antioch he drew attention to it several times in one sermon.[20] At Athens the essence of his message was "Jesus, and the resurrection."[21] When Paul was on trial he declared that the real question was "the hope and resurrection of the dead."[22] Even Festus, the Roman procurator or governor, recognized that the chief thing Paul did was affirm that Jesus is alive.[23]

Surely, in view of this New Testament emphasis, we need to ask ourselves if our preaching, our teaching, and our witness give the same central place to Jesus and the Resurrection. Charles G. Finney, one of the great evangelists of the last century, often said that God frequently uses a neglected truth to bring revival. Perhaps a new emphasis on the Resurrection is what we need today. Who knows what might happen if we gave the Resurrection the place it ought to have in our thinking and in our testimony! The testimony of the first believers never stopped with what God had done for them in saving them, filling

[19] Acts 10:40.
[20] Acts 13:30, 33, 34, 37.
[21] Acts 17:18.
[22] Acts 23:6.
[23] Acts 25:19.

them with the Spirit, healing them, or answering their prayers. Sooner or later they always got around to mentioning the Resurrection.

THE BENEFITS OF THE RESURRECTION

Why was the Resurrection so prominent in their thinking? They realized how much it meant. Because Jesus rose they had salvation and the baptism of the Holy Spirit.[24] Because Jesus rose they could claim God's promise of blessing made to Abraham.[25] It was the risen Christ who brought healing.[26] As long as they gave witness of the Resurrection God gave them miracle-working power "and great grace was upon them all."[27]

Present benefits never made them lose sight of the future, however. As Paul preached before King Agrippa, he asked why it should be thought incredible that God would raise the dead. Then he testified that he himself had seen Jesus, and went on to say: "Having therefore obtained help of God, I continue unto this day, witnessing both to small and great, saying none other things than those which the prophets and Moses did say should come: that Christ should suffer, and that he should be the first that should rise from the dead, and should show light unto the people, and to the Gentiles."[28] The fact that Jesus was the first to rise gives hope that we shall rise. This hope gives the light of understanding, gives meaning and direction to life, not only to Jews, but to Gentiles as well.

The hope of our future resurrection is necessary in order to give full meaning to all the other blessings that are ours through the risen Christ. Physical death

---

[24] Acts 2:38, 39.
[25] Acts 3:25, 26.
[26] Acts 3:15, 16.

[27] Acts 4:33.
[28] Acts 26:22, 23.

does not bring an end to our salvation nor to the work of the Spirit in our lives. Divine healing is more than the restoration of a part that will soon decay again. It is a foretaste of the quickening power of the Resurrection. The guidance we receive for today will not lead us into a dead-end street. We are not mere cogs in a machine soon to be worn out and forgotten. We are fellow-laborers with the Lord, doing His work, carrying His message, walking in the light that will grow brighter and brighter when Jesus comes.

JUDGMENT AND RESTORATION

One of the most outstanding passages in apostolic preaching is found in Acts 3:19-21. "Repent ye therefore, and be converted, that your sins may be blotted out, when the times of refreshing shall come from the presence of the Lord; and he shall send Jesus Christ, which before was preached unto you: whom the heaven must receive until the times of restitution of all things, which God hath spoken by the mouth of all his holy prophets since the world began."

This passage declares Christ's second coming and implies the Resurrection. It also underscores several important truths concerning the present and the future. In the background of these verses is the healing of the lame man at the Gate Beautiful. Peter used this as an opportunity to declare to the temple crowd the glory, holiness, resurrection, and healing power of the Jesus they crucified. The prophets had forewarned them. They should have recognized Jesus as God's Son, as the Prince of Life. Thus, though they crucified Jesus in ignorance, their ignorance was careless, even willful. Peter exhorted them therefore to repent or change their mind and attitudes. He also called on them to be converted or turn back to God so that He might blot out their sins.

God would also do more than forgive their sins. An analysis of this passage shows that the word "when" is translated "that" or "in order that" in most other places (Romans 3:4, for example). They must repent in order that God may send times or appointed seasons of refreshing, relief, strengthening, and revival. They must repent also that God may send Jesus, the appointed Messiah.

Because of the parallelism of the seasons of refreshing and the sending of Jesus, some have supposed that these seasons of refreshing refer to the time when or after Jesus comes. But this is not the case. What Peter is saying is that it is God's immediate and present purpose to send seasons of refreshing and revival on those who repent. He will bring these seasons of revival to a close by sending Jesus. Peter must have had this passage in mind when toward the end of his life he wrote, "The Lord is not slack concerning his promise, as some men count slackness; but is longsuffering to usward, not willing that any should perish, but that all should come to repentance."[29] The apparent delay in Christ's coming is not due to procrastination, but to God's desire for men to repent. He is determined to have a body of people for His name from every nation, tongue, tribe, and people. The implication also is that this age is the age in which men may repent.

Seasons of refreshing and revival are what God has appointed for this age while Christ is in the heavens. When Christ comes again, His purpose will be the "restitution of all things, which God hath

---

[29] 2 Peter 3:9.

spoken by the mouth of all his holy prophets since the world began."[30] That is, Christ's coming will bring in the time for restoring everything that the prophets have prophesied of. The word restitution also implies establishing and fulfillment. It seems to include the whole series of events connected with the second coming of Christ. Peter seems to use it to be the equivalent of the regeneration or renewing spoken of in Matthew 19:28. This time of regeneration includes the twelve apostles sitting on twelve thrones judging or ruling the twelve tribes of Israel. Both these terms, restitution and regeneration or renewing, seem to represent what Jesus also calls "the end of the world,"[31] or consummation, or completion, close, implies fulfillment, just as these other terms do. They summarize the whole period of the Second Coming.

Part of the fulfillment will be judgment. The resurrection of Jesus guarantees the fulfillment of all the prophecies. The risen Christ will be the Judge of the quick, that is, the living, and the dead.[32] The Resurrection is the assurance that God really has "appointed a day, in the which he will judge the world in righteousness by that man whom he hath ordained," that is, Jesus.[33]

When the governor Felix came to Paul to listen to what Paul had to say about faith in Christ, literally "the in-Christ faith," Paul discussed three phases. First was the subject of righteousness. If we examine other things Paul said, this means Paul talked about the need for righteousness and the fact that none are righteous in themselves. Then he explained the righteousness that is ours by grace through faith in Jesus,

---

[30] Acts 3:21.
[31] Matthew 13:39, 40; 24:3; 28:20.
[32] Acts 10:40, 42.
[33] Acts 17:31; 24:15.

a righteousness that is His and which is made ours because He died and rose again. God looks at us "in Christ" just as if we had never sinned.

Second, Paul spoke of temperance or self-control. This is part of the fruit of the Spirit, a very necessary part if our lives are to be directed as God wills, and if we are to have the wholeness and holiness without which no man can see God.

Third, he spoke of judgment to come, warning him of the wrath that must come on all who reject Jesus.

The Book of Acts does not end on a note of judgment, however. Its final words tell how Paul for two years in Rome "received all that came in unto him, preaching the kingdom of God, and teaching those things which concern the Lord Jesus Christ."[34] The hope of the gospel is the Kingdom. The center of that hope is the King.

[34] Acts 28:30, 31.

QUESTIONS

1. What did Jesus seek to teach His disciples during the forty days He spent on earth after His resurrection?

2. Why did Jesus turn the attention of the disciples away from the time of His coming to the work to be done?

3. Was it important for the disciples to see Jesus ascend? Why?

4. Why did the apostles in their preaching say more about the Resurrection than about heaven?

5. What are some of the benefits of the Resurrection emphasized in apostolic preaching?

6. What did the apostles emphasize in order to encourage repentance?

5 ROMANS
Good News of God's Love

THE DAY OF JUDGMENT

The Book of Acts mentions frequently that Paul preached, taught, "disputing and persuading the things concerning the kingdom of God."[1] The word "disputing" is translated "reasoned" in Acts 18:19. The basic meaning is simply to conduct a discussion with a view to persuading people of the truth. The Book of Acts does not say much about how these were carried on. Acts is a very much condensed story. Sermons that may have taken hours are recorded sometimes in only a few words. But when Paul wrote to the Romans, he had not yet visited them. So he conducted one of his discussions in the letter, even to the point of bringing up objections and then answering them. The Epistle to the Romans shows us how the Spirit used Paul to deal with people who knew little about the gospel and how he led them along to a full and deep knowledge.

At Athens, the Book of Acts shows that Paul did not talk to sinners about the Second Coming as such. Instead, he drew their attention to their need for repentance. Then he reinforced this by telling them of the Day of Judgment, a day we can be sure will come because God raised His Son from the dead.

[1] Acts 19:8.

57

Writing to the Romans in another great Gentile city, Paul follows something of the same line. He declares his call to be an apostle separated unto the gospel of God. This gospel is good news concerning Jesus who rose from the dead and was thus declared to be the powerful Son of God. Then, beginning with Romans 1:18, Paul deals in detail with the fact that all men need the gospel.

Paul first addresses the Gentiles. In the gospel is the revelation that the wrath of God will come from heaven on men who hold the truth in unrighteousness. The word "hold" means to hold down, hold back, suppress. The righteousness of God is the standard. Because men fall short, they need to repent. But godless men suppress the truth about God's righteousness and encourage men to continue to live in sin. Instead of accepting the truth about God, they became vain and proud in their imaginations or thoughts, reasonings, and philosophizing. All this theorizing led them away from God. Soon they were substituting the worship of unworthy objects for the worship of the true God. They exalted themselves and soon worshiped creatures instead of the Creator. Because God is righteous, His wrath and judgment must come upon all those who reject the truth and follow empty theories.

It may seem strange that the Day of Judgment and the outpouring of God's wrath are here put as part of the good news, the gospel. But Paul sees it as good news because he sees the results of all this proud, vain theorizing that leaves the true God out. It led to vile and unnatural lusts, to all kinds of immorality, covetousness, malice, envy, murder, lies. Read the list of Romans 1:26-32. It pictures a complete moral breakdown, brought on by a godless intelligentsia who take pleasure in destroying the standards of righteousness God has given and who are not satisfied unless they drag others down the same road they are going. It is good news that God's wrath will fall on that sort of unrighteousness. But the very purpose of the gospel is to save men from that wrath.

Though modern men do not worship idols, they still put human reason on the throne and worship the creature instead of the Creator. Modern theorizing and godless philosophies are bringing about the same sort of moral breakdown. If Paul were here today, he would have little to say to the world at large about the Second Coming as such. He would not begin by broadcasting the good news of the joy and glory of Christ's return. He would talk about the Day of Judgment. He would not begin by talking about the love of God. He would warn of the wrath to come. Too many today have watered down the love of God until God sounds like a little old grandmother sitting in a corner passing out candy suckers. God's love for man is so great that He cannot allow ungodliness, unrighteousness, and the godless theories of intellectuals to go on forever dragging men down. He would not be fair, just, righteous, or loving if He did.

Paul did not stop with God's wrath on the wicked, however. He went on to show that good, moral, religious people who worship the one true God also need the gospel. He had in mind the Jews of his day, but what he says applies to other religious people. They used their religion to judge and criticize others. They made their boast in God and set themselves up as guides and teachers. Yet all too often they did the very things they preached against and brought dishonor on the name of God. Their past blessings and privilege would not exempt them from judgment. Sometimes they thought they were eternally secure because they proclaimed the truth. They did not recognize that God was just being merciful and long-suffering, giving them opportunity to repent. Some thought that because God was still blessing them He was excusing their secret sins. What they were really doing was despising His goodness that was meant to lead them to repentance, and laying up for themselves a store of wrath which would be poured out on them in that day when God will reveal His righteous judgment.

Here Paul emphasizes again that God's judgment will be just, rendering "to every man according to his deeds."[2] As in the parables and teaching of Jesus, there will be just two classes. On one side are those who do good, having received God's grace. They "by patient continuance in well-doing seek for glory and honour and immortality" or incorruption.[3] The result for them, whether Jew or Gentile, will be eternal life which includes glory, honour, and peace.

On the other side will be those who do evil, having rejected God's call. They are contentious. The Greek word indicates that the cause of their contentiousness and strife, is selfishness and selfish ambition. They do not obey the truth. Instead they obey unrighteousness. The result for them will be divine indignation and wrath which includes tribulation or suffering and anguish.[4] The Day of God will be a day when God reveals the secrets of men. The impartial judge will be Jesus. The impartial standard will be the gospel.[5] All men stand guilty. Therefore all men need the

2 Romans 2:6.   4 Romans 2:8, 9.
3 Romans 2:7.   5 Romans 2:16.

salvation the gospel tells us God has provided through Christ. Christ will be the Judge in the Judgment Day. But men must not wait to accept His salvation until then.

What Paul says reminds us a little of the Book of Amos. The prosperous Israelites took their prosperity as a sign of God's blessing and they talked a great deal about the coming Day of the Lord. But Amos told them that because of their careless sins, their unconcern over God's people, their love of luxury and their disregard of the needs of others, the Day of the Lord would be darkness and not light. There would be no brightness in it for them.[6] So today, it will take more than talking about the coming of the Lord to be ready.

THE ASSURANCE OF GLORY

After showing that all men need the salvation which the gospel proclaims, Paul goes on to show that the gospel means justification by faith, deliverance from sin, and sharing the glory of God. Because we are justified (treated as righteous) by faith, we have peace, access to God, and a joy that exults in the hope of the glory of God.[7] The assurance of this to our hearts is the resurrection of Jesus. If God loved us enough to send His Son to die for us while we were sinners, enemies, rebels, now that Jesus is alive and has made us God's friends surely God will see us all the way through to glory.[8]

Some have interpreted this to mean that once we are saved we can slide the rest of the way into heaven. But this passage does not mean that we can do as we please and still get into heaven. What it says is that

[6] Amos 5:18, 20.   [8] Romans 5:8, 9.
[7] Romans 5:1, 2.

God's love has made full provision for our salvation. God's love has also made full provision for taking us all the way to glory. But just as we must appropriate salvation by faith, so we must continue to appropriate God's provision for us with the same active, obedient faith. By faith we continue to be "in Christ" in vital, up-to-date, living experience. This union with Christ gives us power to live a holy life, power to overcome, power to dedicate and keep dedicated our whole beings to Him. Thus, through Christ's merit and mediation we shall escape the judgment which will come on the wicked, and we shall enter into glory.

Chapter six removes all doubt that we must fully appropriate God's provision if we are to share the glory. We are under grace, but that does not mean we can live in lawlessness. God has set us free from the old law so that we can accept new responsibilities, so that we can make Christ the Lord of our lives. If we serve sin we will still end in shame and death. Only if we obey Christ and serve righteousness will we know the glory that comes with eternal life.

Chapter eight emphasizes two basic conditions for entering into the glory with Christ, to be glorified with Him. They are sonship and suffering.

As sons we are no longer in a state of bondage, slaves to the desires of the flesh and the mind. As sons we have life through the work of the Holy Spirit. Christ lives in us. His Spirit dwells in us, and God gives us assurance that He will quicken or resurrect our mortal bodies by His Spirit. We mortify or put to death the selfish, fleshly deeds of the body because we are led of the Spirit. And because we are led of the Spirit we are sons.

As sons also, we are in a state of adoption. In

Rome wealthy children were brought up frugally and strictly, kept under tutors, and treated little better than slaves. But when they became of age they received the "adoption," or the "placing" of sons. That is, they entered into the full rights and privileges which were theirs because of their sonship. As Christians we do not have to wait until the Resurrection to receive the adoption. We are sons now. We can claim the privileges of sonship now. We can begin to act like sons now. As we begin to do so, the Holy Spirit bears witness to our sonship by causing us to cry out to God in worship, recognizing Him as our Father. (When Paul says we cry, Abba, Father, he was recognizing both Jews and Gentiles in this state of adoption. The Jews would cry out Abba, which is Father in their language. The Gentiles would cry out Father in their own language.) This assurance that we are sons carries with it the assurance that we are heirs, joint-heirs with Christ, sharing an inheritance promised to the Seed of Abraham, sharing a glory that belongs to the Son of God.

Paul, at this point, does not spend a great deal of time talking about the other condition for sharing the glory. We must share Christ's sufferings. But the glory will be so great, it will so far outbalance the sufferings that the sufferings are hardly worth mentioning.

In view of all the suffering in the world, this might sound overoptimistic. It is easy in revival to think of the Lord's coming and bubble over with enthusiasm. But after the emotional tide recedes, what do we have left to assure us that the glory will be real? Paul says we have our groanings, our inner expectancy and hope, and the help of the Holy Spirit.

We share our groanings with all creation. Man is
a part of God's creation. When man sinned, nature
was brought under a curse so that it did not yield as
it should. Nature is full of futility and incomplete-
ness. Nature does not seem to have an aim or direction
anymore. But when Jesus comes and we receive the
redemption of our bodies (new creations, just as the
redemption of our spirits meant, we became new
creatures), all nature will be put right. The lion will
lie down with the lamb. The desert will blossom as a
rose.

The fact that faith causes hope to spring within us
also assures us that there is more ahead. If we in
this life already had all God has for us, why would
there be this consciousness of hope? God has given us
this hope to help us be patient and endure the tests
and the waiting for the salvation, the glory that is
still ahead.

In our infirmities or weakness, we do not know how
to pray or what to pray for to help us enter into the
privileges of our sonship now, nor how we can accomplish God's will in suffering so that we can be
glorified with Christ. But the Spirit knows. He helps
us. He makes intercession for us. And because He
knows the will of God, we know that His prayer will
be answered and God will work all things together
for our good.

What is this will of God that means our good, what
is that good that God has for us? Paul points us back
to God's foreknowledge. God knew when He called
Abraham that in Abraham and in Abraham's seed
(Christ) all the families of the earth would be
blessed.[9] Then He predestined or foreordained that

_____
[9] Genesis 12:3.

the blessing would take the form of sonship, a sonship in which Christ would have the leadership among many who are conformed to His image, made like Him, justified now, to be glorified when He comes. This glorification is so sure that Paul puts it in the past tense, "Them he also glorified."[10] It is as good as done.

Chapter four showed that our relationship with God is by grace through faith. God formed His plan in eternity. He extends His call and works out His plan now through those who respond in faith. Our part is to hear the call and obey it. We do not have to glorify ourselves. If we follow Christ by the Spirit in the path of sonship and suffering, God will glorify us. The love that sent Jesus to Calvary will enable us to be more than conquerors. No misfortune, no enemy seen or unseen, nothing in life or death, nothing in earth or heaven can separate us from that love. We still have a choice. As long as we choose to walk the road of sonship and suffering in simple, obedient faith, we cannot miss the goal, we cannot be robbed of the glory. This much is foreordained.

GOD'S PURPOSE OF RESTORATION

In Romans 9-11, Paul deals with the future of the Jews. The question comes to mind, "If God is going to do all this for the Gentiles, what does this do to His promises to the Jews?" Paul, after declaring his own concern for the salvation of his brothers in the flesh, affirms that God will be faithful to His promises. This faithfulness is seen now in that a remnant are now being saved. It will be seen in the future by the full restoration of national Israel.

---

[10] Romans 8:30.

The rejection of Christ by the Jews made it impossible for God to continue to use them as channels of His Spirit and blessing. God did not cause this. But it forced the Jewish believers to turn to the Gentiles as Paul did on his first missionary journey.[11] This became an opportunity for the spread of the gospel to the world. Paul uses an illustration here. The Jews were like natural branches cut out of an olive tree; the Gentiles, like wild branches grafted into the tree. But God's purpose is restoration. He will graft the Jews back in when they believe in Jesus. God's purpose is actually a full restoration and a full number for both Jew and Gentile. However, only a remnant, a small number, can be expected from the Jews now. Not until after the full number of Gentiles is complete can we expect the revival and restoration God has promised for Israel. This clearly points to the time at the end of the age, the time of the events which are in direct connection with the second coming of Christ.

Two questions often arise in connection with chapter eleven of Romans. First, what is meant by "All Israel shall be saved"?[12] The words "and so" connect it with the preceding verse which speaks of "the fulness of the Gentiles." This means all the Gentiles who believe. It seems reasonable therefore to take the next verse to mean all Israel who believe. Paul has already said in this letter that no Jew will be saved just because he is a Jew.[13] But God will have a full number of believers from both Jews and Gentiles.

The other question has to do with Romans 11:29, "The gifts and calling of God are without repentance."

---

[11] Acts 13:45, 46.   [13] Romans 2:28, 29.
[12] Romans 11:26.

The word repentance means a changing of the mind. God offers a gift or calling and He does not change His mind and withdraw it just because some do not believe. Once they are given they are always available. The fact that Jews did not believe means now both Jews and Gentile are both in unbelief. But God's mercy is therefore extended to both. The gifts and callings once enjoyed by the Jews are available to both. God will have mercy on all who believe.

THE LAW OF LOVE

The concluding section of the Book of Romans is full of practical exhortations for Christian living. In all of these love is the one great obligation, the one thing we owe and must keep on owing.[14] We can never love enough to outbalance the love God has given us. What Christ has done for us is not the only motivation for our love, however. We are to be full of love because we know the time (that is, we know the season). We know that this is the age before Christ's return. "For now is our salvation nearer than when we believed."[15]

If we really believe that Jesus is coming and that a new day will dawn, this will give us tremendous motivation to do several things in our Christian experience:

1. To be awake, vibrant, dynamic in our love.

2. To put off the works of darkness (evil and ignorance) so that we can put on the armor of the light of the knowledge of our Lord and Saviour Jesus Christ.

3. We will walk honestly, as in the day. This means we will not have any room in our lives for rioting, or excessive feasting, or carousing, or revelry. It will mean no drunkenness or dissipation; no chambering or sexual excesses; no wantonness or indecent

---

[14] Romans 13:8.   [15] Romans 13:11.

conduct; no strife, discord, contention, quarrels; and no envying or jealousy. Instead, we will put on Christ, making no provision for, and not taking care of, the wrong desires which arise out of our physical natures.

4. We will avoid despising a person who is so weak in the faith that he is upset by nonessentials such as the kind of food he eats. When we look ahead to the kingdom of God we know that the things that prepare us are not what we eat or drink, but righteousness, peace, and joy in the Holy Spirit. Love and faith expressed in the light of Christ's coming will help us put up with the infirmities of the weak that keep him from eating certain foods or that make him depend on other things as props for his faith. Instead of pleasing ourselves in such matters, we will follow Christ's example of self-denial and will find comfort and encouragement in the prophetic word that gives us hope for the future.

We can sum it up by saying that Romans assures us of glory through a gospel that brings us faith, hope, and love.

QUESTIONS

1. Why does Paul emphasize judgment in the first part of the Epistle to the Romans?

2. What are some of the facts Romans teaches about future judgment and about the way it will be conducted?

3. What assurance does Romans give us that it is God's purpose to bring us to glory?

4. What are the two basic conditions for entering into glory with Christ?

5. What assures us that the glory will be real?

6. How is God now showing His faithfulness to His promises given in the Old Testament to Israel? How will He show His faithfulness in the future?

7. If we really believe that Jesus is coming, what should this stir us to do?

6 Living in the Light of His Coming

THE CLIMAX OF OUR FAITH

Paul knew the Corinthians well. He spent a year and a half with them. He knew their needs, their weaknesses, their problems, their sins, their failures. Yet he starts out his letter to them by saying some tremendous and wonderful things about them.

They are an assembly or church of God's free citizens. They are sanctified, set apart, dedicated, consecrated in and by Christ Jesus. They are called to be saints, "with all that in every place call upon the name of Jesus."[1] "Calling on the name" also means called over to His name, belonging to Him and called by His name. "Called to be saints" is present, not future. The idea is, the Corinthian believers along with all others wherever they are who belong to Jesus are saints (consecrated, dedicated people) who have answered God's call to salvation, service, and eternal life.

Jesus has given them the grace and favor of God and made them rich. These rich possessions are by and in Christ, depending on Him and on our close relationship with Him. They include all utterance or the full word (Greek, *logos*), that is, the full gospel; along with all or every kind of knowledge necessary to confirm the testimony of Jesus and prove it reliable in

[1] 1 Corinthians 1:2.

69

their own experience. As a result, the Corinthians were not lacking in any of the spiritual gifts which are so freely given by God's grace.

All of these blessings are, however, neither the sum total nor the object of their faith. They are given as evidences of God's grace while the believers wait eagerly for the coming or revelation, disclosure, revealing (Greek, *apokalypsis,* translated "manifestation" in Romans 8:19) of our Lord Jesus. God's blessings and gifts are also means by which He will continue to confirm, strengthen, and establish us so that we will be blameless and without fault in the day of our Lord Jesus.

In this passage Paul is using the revelation of our Lord Jesus as a general term for His coming parallel with the "day of our Lord Jesus Christ."[2] The "day of our Lord Jesus" is used again in 2 Corinthians 1:14 as a general term for all the various events which will take place in connection with the Second Coming. The important thing is that we wait eagerly for His coming, with our attention on Him, seeking Him now for the strength we need so that on that day it will be clear that Jesus truly has taken away all our sin and guilt. Then, at His coming, we shall be revealed as the sons of God.[3] As John puts it, "Beloved, now are we the sons of God, and it doth not yet appear what we shall be: but we know that, when he shall appear [be revealed], we shall be like him; for we shall see him as he is."[4]

The second coming of Christ is therefore the climax of our faith. Those who have heeded God's call and been made rich in the knowledge and experience of

[2] 1 Corinthians 1:8.   [4] 1 John 3:2.
[3] Romans 8:19.

the full gospel cannot help but wait eagerly for His coming. New Testament Christianity must be lived in the light and expectation of Christ's return. To the degree that any church or individual minimizes or neglects that hope, to that degree they have drifted from the full gospel of our Lord Jesus Christ. They can have everything else, but if that hope has become dim they are no longer truly Pentecostal. The Spirit, who knows the deep things of God, wants to focus our attention on those things God has prepared for us. This is foreign to the natural man, the man whose chief concern is life on earth. He has never seen, heard, or even imagined anything as wonderful as what God has for us. But those who have the Holy Spirit find that He loves to reveal these hidden depths of God's purpose to us.[5]

WE SHALL BE JUDGED

After such a wonderful introduction it seems strange that Paul soon begins to talk about judgment. We saw in Acts and in Romans that Paul made judgment a chief emphasis when talking to sinners and heathen who did not understand the wonderful plan of God. But Paul says he cannot talk any more about the glory and mystery of Christ's coming because the Corinthians were not acting like Spirit-filled men and women. Instead, they were like carnal folk. They looked at things the way the world does. They were like babes in Christ because they were no longer fully surrendered to the working of the Spirit. They were living like men of the world, full of jealousy, strife, quarrels, cliques, and party spirit.

The Corinthians seemed to have forgotten that the foundation of their Christian life was Jesus Christ

[5] 1 Corinthians 2:9, 10, 13, 14.

Himself. Some were building on that foundation with
gold, silver, and precious stones. That is, they were
doing work for God using the valuable gifts of His
grace. Others were using wood, hay, stubble, and
other worthless stuff unworthy of the wonderful
foundation. Instead of seeking Christ's glory, they
were moved by unworthy motives, self-seeking, pride,
and anger. They were more concerned about building
up their own name or building up their own clique or
party than building for God. *Faithfulness*

Sometimes the tests of this life will reveal the
quality of our work. More often, it will take the tests
of the Day of Christ to show them up. In that day
there will be a fire which will show whether these
works are gold, silver, and precious stones, or wood,
hay, and stubble.

Paul deals with the same subject in 2 Corinthians
5:9, 10. He says that whether he is at home or away,
(which may mean, whether he lives or dies) he makes
it his one ambition to be acceptable to the Lord, for
we must all appear or be revealed before the judgment
seat of Christ to receive a reward for what we have
done (accomplished, or made a practice of doing,
busied ourselves with) while in the body. Here, the
"judgment seat" is one word in the Greek. It was
actually a throne such as the winners of the Olympic
games appeared before to get their awards. (An en-
tirely different word is used of the great white throne
of judgment in Revelation 20:11.)

Only Christians appear before this judgment seat
or throne of Christ. Paul is talking to Christians.
He includes Himself. There it will be shown that
some things we do for the Lord are good, right, useful,
and fit for reward. Other things will be revealed to be

bad or worthless, that is, wood, hay, stubble.

What is it that makes a work done for Christ worthless? First Corinthians 13 gives the answer. If we speak with tongues of men and angels and have not charity (a high, holy, self-giving love), we are like the jingling brass and clanging cymbals used by the heathen to accompany their wails to false gods. That is, our tongues are worthless, just meaningless noise. They do not accomplish any edification for us or others. If we have the gift of prophecy, understand all kinds of mysteries, and have all kinds of knowledge, even if we are so full of faith we can remove mountains, and have not love, we are nothing. Which means that what we do is worthless and meaningless. If we dole out all our belongings to the poor, and even if we give our bodies to be burned at the stake as martyrs and have not love it profits or benefits us in no way. That is, we will have no reward.

By this, we see also that the judgment throne of Christ is not for judging our sins, nor does it have anything to do with our eternal salvation. Only the saved will appear before Christ there to have their works tested for the sake of receiving the proper reward. The sad fact is that some will find all their works worthless. They will be like a man saved out of a fire, but able to save none of his possessions. They will be utterly without reward.

The Roman Catholics sometimes used 1 Corinthians 3:15 as a proof text for their doctrine of purgatory. But the fire affects the works, not the Christians. Furthermore, the fire takes place at the time of the judgment seat of Christ, which is after He comes for the Church and catches it away to be with Him. It has nothing to do with the present time or with the time between death and the Day of Judgment.

In view of the seriousness of the judgment seat or throne of Christ, it is no wonder that Paul aspired in everything to be acceptable and pleasing to Christ. The coming judgment made him know also a "terror," actually, a fear, reverence, and respect for the Lord and also made him try to persuade men to serve God and others from the heart.[6]

The same spirit will keep us from pride, boasting, empty intellectualism, or any honoring of human leaders that would lead to party spirit or strife. Instead, we would realize that the contributions men make belong to us, as do all things God has provided for us in this world and the next. But we belong to Christ, so we must use everything to build for God, without taking any credit to ourselves. We are God's building. The growth, the progress, the blessing are all from Him.

Paul draws one other important lesson from the coming judgment at the judgment seat of Christ. Since it will take the fire of that judgment to test our works to see whether they are gold, silver, and precious stones or wood, hay, and stubble, we are foolish to try to judge the work and motives of one another now. He alone can bring to light what is hidden in darkness (not sins, but the hidden motives that do not show on the outside). He alone can make manifest or reveal the counsels or motives of the heart. We must therefore be careful not to judge anything before the appointed time, that is, before we appear at the judgment seat. Paul did not even judge himself with continuous self-examination, for he knew that even when he was conscious of nothing wrong, this did not justify

---

[6] 2 Corinthians 5:11-13.

Him. He too would have to submit everything to the judgment of the Lord.[7]

The command not to pass judgment on others must not be carried too far, however. It applies to what others do for the Lord. It does not apply to their sins. The Corinthians were, in fact, tolerating a very serious sin in their midst, where a man was living with his stepmother. Even the Gentiles would not tolerate that kind of immorality, but the Corinthian Christians were so taken up with promoting their cliques and so taken up with strife that they were paying no attention to this sin. This was not fair to Christ because it gave outsiders the wrong idea of what Christianity stands for. It was not fair to the church, because such tolerating of sin would be like a leaven or yeast spreading through a lump of dough. Soon one and then another would begin to let down their standards and who knows what immorality might erupt in the church?

Most important, it was not fair to the man who was sinning. He needed to be dealt with by handing him over to Satan to bring destruction on his body, that is, physical suffering, that his spirit might be saved in the Judgment Day, the Day of the Lord Jesus.

Paul further explains that this means putting the man out of their group, cutting him off from their fellowship. The object was to make him realize that he was no longer a member of the body of Christ but was again under subjection to Satan, the prince of this world.[8] The hope then was that in his suffering he would realize his condition, repent, and seek the Lord for restoration. The evidence is that the man

---

[7] 1 Corinthians 4:3-5.   [8] John 12:31; Romans 6:16.

did just that, but the church was slow to forgive and
restore him to fellowship. Paul had to write and tell
them that he forgave the man and they ought to also.
More than that, they should comfort or encourage him
and confirm or reaffirm their love for him, "lest
perhaps such a one should be swallowed up [or over-
whelmed, drowned]" by extreme sorrow (or grief over
his sins and over the loss of Christian fellowship) .'
Failure of the church to forgive would give Satan
just as big an advantage as the man's sin did before.

We Shall Judge Others

To most folk today the Second Coming and the
Judgment are away off in the future. The Second
Coming may encourage them to live for the Lord, but
they seldom think of it in connection with the practical
problems of everyday life. This was not so for Paul.
What God has for us in the future was for him an
important and constant guide for every situation that
might arise in this life. We see an example of this
when we see how Paul dealt with Corinthian believers who were going to law before unjust heathen
judges.

Corinth, the capital of the Roman province of
Achaia or Greece, was an extremely immoral city. Its
habits and practices so shocked even their pagan
neighbors that they invented a new word, "to Co-
rinthianize," which meant to indulge in the basest
kind of lust and sin. How could Christians expect
justice by going before such judges? How much better
it would be if they brought their problems before the
church. Even the least esteemed Christian would be
able to do a better job than these heathen judges.

' 2 Corinthians 2:7, (8-11).

By going to heathen courts of law, the Christians were also forgetting something very important. They would some day judge the world and angels as well. Surely, there must be someone among them wise enough to judge the little problems of this life.

Actually, it was an utter defeat for them to go to the law at all.[10] It would be better for them to be wronged, defrauded, robbed, and suffer it. But they must also remember that by doing any wrong or injury to their Christian brother, or by holding back anything that belongs to him, they are putting themselves in the same class as the unjust in the world. In fact, if they continue in any of the old sins they could not receive God's kingdom.

In a similar vein, Paul draws attention to the punishment of the Israelites in the wilderness for their lust, immorality, and critical spirit. God meant them as examples for us. Their history did not have to be written down for their sakes, but for ours. We need the warning because we face the end of the ages. We are in the final age before Christ comes to bring God's plan to its consummation.[11] The world seems to think time will go on forever. The fact is, we do not have much time left. It is time that we began to live with the end time in view. We should not be so occupied with the things of this world, so tied down to the cares and ambitions of this life, that we cannot bear to leave them long enough to do the work God has called us to do. If we do not quit making the things of this life our chief concern, if we do not learn to hold the things of this life loosely, we may find ourselves left behind in their grip when Jesus comes.

---

[10] 1 Corinthians 6:7, (8-10).   [11] 1 Corinthians 10:11.

WE SHALL BE RAISED

Not all in Corinth were concerned about material things. It seems that some went too far in the other direction. They considered themselves so advanced and so spiritual that they did not need to be concerned about the body. This led on one hand to immorality, and on the other to a denial of the resurrection of the body.

Some took it that since Christ had set them free, they were free to do anything. They argued that their spirits were saved and it was a matter of indifference what they ate or drank or how they indulged the body.

Paul agreed that all things are lawful, we are free to do anything.[12] At first, this may seem strange, since Paul has just said that those who continue in their old sins cannot inherit the Kingdom. But Paul quickly qualifies his statement. He is allowed to do anything, but not everything is expedient, that is, useful, helpful, or good for something. Paul implies he would not waste his time or money on such things when there is so much to do for the Lord. Furthermore, Paul would not use his freedom in a way that would cause him to lose it. He refused to indulge in anything that would enslave him. This certainly rules out the habits and addictions so common in the world today. These things that enslave are contradictory to the principle of Christian liberty.

As far as "meats" or good food are concerned, Paul is free. Food and the stomach are made for each other. At the end time God will destroy or, as the Greek word indicates, do away with both and release us from both. To eat or not to eat does not affect our spiritual destiny. But fornication or immorality is not

---

[12] 1 Corinthians 6:12.

a matter that can be treated with the same indifference. The body was made for food, but the body was not made for immorality. Furthermore, the Lord is for the body; that is, He is concerned about the body. This is proved by the fact that He raised Jesus, not merely spiritually, but in an actual, bodily resurrection. It is proved also by the fact that He will use His power to resurrect us also. Not only so, He paid a price for us. The blood of Jesus was shed that we might belong to Him, body, soul, mind, and spirit.

Those in Corinth who denied that our bodies will be raised (perhaps they were influenced by heathen philosophies taught in their universities) were involving themselves in a contradiction. As Christians, they confessed that God raised Jesus from the dead. But Jesus in His death took our place. He died as a man. If we are not raised, then He was not, and all who have died trusting in Christ are now in hell. But Christ actually was raised, literally, "out from among the dead."[13] Because of spiritual union with Christ by faith, they that are His will be raised at His coming.[14] Then, after that, will come the end when Christ will vanquish every enemy including physical death. That is, the rest of the dead will be raised. Revelation 20 shows that this third stage will take place after the Millennium. This compares with John 5:28, 29; Matthew 27:52, 53; and Daniel 12:2; all of which indicate two separate resurrections, one for the righteous, the other for the wicked.

WE SHALL BE CHANGED

Our body retains its identity even though it is said that all the chemical elements in it are replaced at least every seven years. So our body will retain

---

[13] 1 Corinthians 15:20.   [14] 1 Corinthians 15:23.

its identity in the Resurrection. But we will be clothed upon with a new creation God has for us. As the wheat plant is the same "it" as the seed that was buried, yet is vastly different, so will it be with us. Our bodies sown in corruption, perishable, deteriorating, decaying, will be raised in incorruption, not subject to decay or death anymore. Buried in a state of humiliation and weakness, they will be raised in glory and power. Buried as natural bodies "of the earth, earthy,"[15] that is, suited for earthly, natural life, they will be raised as spiritual bodies like Christ's. This does not mean our new bodies will be unreal or ghostly. They will be just as real as our present bodies are, but perfectly suited to express the heavenly life we shall enjoy in the coming Kingdom.

What will happen to those who are still alive when the trumpet of the Lord sounds and the resurrection of the dead in Christ takes place? At the same instant they will be changed, clothed upon with the same immortal, incorruptible bodies, never to know sin, decay, or death again. Other things will pass away then too, even some good things such as tongues and prophecy which have their primary purpose to give edification during the present church age.[16]

Now, in addition to the fact of Christ's resurrection, we have another guarantee that God will do all this for us. The Holy Spirit is an earnest, first installment, or "token payment in advance" of the glory to come.[17] The Holy Spirit also prepares us for that time when we will be clothed upon with our new body that is subject only to life and not death.[18]

[15] 1 Corinthians 15:47.
[16] 1 Corinthians 13:8-10.
[17] 2 Corinthians 1:22.
[18] 2 Corinthians 5:4, 5.

All this gives the Christian the greatest encouragement in suffering. He can afford to risk his life because he knows he will not lose anything. He will be raised. He will share in an eternal weight of glory that will make the past seem as nothing, where "I die daily" means "I face death every day, I risk my life every day in the work of the Lord."[19]

This gives us further encouragement to service. We labor or aspire to be acceptable to the Lord in order to receive that eternal weight of glory. We seek to be steadfast or firm in faith, immovable from our hope, always abounding or growing and seeking to excel in the work of the Lord, for we know that our work, labor, trouble, and difficulty are not in vain in the Lord.[20] Nothing we do or suffer for Him is ever fruitless or is ever wasted. What greater incentive for service or protection from instability could we have than the promise of His coming?

---

[19] 1 Corinthians 15:30-32. (See also 2 Corinthians 4:17, 18.) [20] 1 Corinthians 15:58.

QUESTIONS

1. What are some of the blessings and gifts which prepare us for Christ's coming?

2. For what purpose will Christians be judged? On what basis will we be judged?

3. Why did Paul exhort the Corinthians not to take spiritual matters to secular court?

4. What practical effects should the Second Coming have on our present lives and relationships?

5. Discuss the two separate resurrections. Give Scripture to support your answer.

6. What will be the nature of the Resurrection and of our new bodies?

7 Encouragement to Holiness

CHILDREN OF GOD'S PROMISE

Some of Paul's epistles were written to meet specific problems in the churches. Sometimes little is said about the Second Coming because the solution to the problem is more closely related to some other truth. But the Second Coming was never left out altogether. For Paul and for all the Early Church, it was always in view. Paul's Letter to the Galatians is an example.

Paul wrote Galatians to deal with the arguments of the Judaizers. These converted Pharisees taught that Gentiles could only have full standing before God if they came through the door of Judaism. They must first accept the Old Covenant, accept circumcision, and obey the forms of the old Law before they could claim all the promises of God.

Paul showed them the foolishness of any attempt to keep the old Law by pointing to the Scripture and to their experiences. How did they receive the Holy Spirit? Not by doing what the Law said, but by responding to the message of the gospel in simple faith.[1] Abraham pleased God and received the promise by the same simple faith. The Law was "added because of transgressions, till the seed should come to whom

[1] Galatians 3:2.

82

the promise was made."[2] The "seed" or descendant of Abraham to come was Christ. Through Christ alone is the fulfillment of the promise given to Abraham that "in thee and in thy seed shall all the families of the earth be blessed."[3] The Law's work was only preparatory. It acted like a schoolmaster or tutor to stand over the people and teach them some lessons and to guide them through the centuries until Christ would come. Once Christ came, the Law's work was finished, fulfilled, and now our relationship to God is through simple faith in Jesus. We are His children, we have put on Christ. All believers, no matter what our background, race, social condition, or sex, are one in Christ Jesus.[4] And because we are in Christ, who is the true Seed of Abraham[5] the true heir of the promise, then we too become Abraham's seed (in Christ), heirs of God, sure to receive the same promise.

To illustrate this in another way, Paul compares those who put themselves under the Law to children of Hagar (Abraham and Sarah's handmaid), slaves, and those who accept God's promise in faith to children of Sarah, free. He also compares Hagar and these Judaizers to Mount Sinai and the earthly Jerusalem, in bondage and slavery, while true believers are free sons of the heavenly Jerusalem. This illustration also shows how the Second Coming continually directed Paul's thinking. The Judaizers looked back. Their attention was focused on the past, on Mount Sinai. Paul looked ahead and focused his attention of the freedom and sonship which we will enjoy to the full in the New Jerusalem.[6]

---

[2] Galatians 3:19.
[3] Genesis 12:3.
[4] Galatians 3:28.

[5] Galatians 3:16.
[6] Galatians 4:26.

The latter part of Galatians is full of exhortations to keep the people from misunderstanding what Paul says about freedom. To the heathen, freedom meant license, freedom to do whatever they felt like doing. But freedom from the Law does not mean freedom to sin. Paul points them ahead to the future Kingdom. They cannot inherit the Kingdom if they follow the indecent desires of human nature, the "works of the flesh."[7] Those truly free are those who are loosed from the power of the old nature because the Holy Spirit is in control. Love and all the fruit of the Spirit will mark those who are led by the Spirit, who are heirs with Christ, who will receive the Kingdom and everything else that God has promised.

God's Eternal Purpose

Paul wrote Ephesians while he was for two years under house arrest in Rome. There, his mind dwelt on the plan of God, and the Holy Spirit gave him new insights into the mystery of God's purpose and the glory to come. He wrote Ephesians, not to meet any particular problem, but to strengthen and encourage the Christians.

Why has God blessed us with heavenly, spiritual blessings in Christ? Why has He chosen that we should be holy and without blame before Him in love, having the place and privileges of children, accepted and blessed, redeemed and forgiven in and through His Beloved Son? His one great purpose is "that in the dispensation of the fulness of times he might gather together in one all things in Christ, both which are in heaven, and which are on earth; even in him: in whom also we have obtained an inheritance."[8]

Dispensation is a word meaning "management,"

---

[7] Galatians 5:19-21.   [8] Ephesians 1:10, 11.

and implies a plan and arrangements for carrying it out. "The fulness of times"[9] is a phrase used of harvest or completion, or of the time itself being ripe. The idea, then, seems to be that when the time is right God will bring everything together in heaven and earth with Christ as the Head. The same word translated "dispensation" is translated "fellowship" in Ephesians 3:9. There, Paul goes on to show that this eternal purpose which God is carrying out through Christ is being made known now through the Church.

The important point here for our study of the Second Coming is that God's purpose will continue to center in His dealings with and through the Church. It is in and through the Church that God is bringing together all things in Christ. He is doing it now. He will continue to do so in the future. This is because God has appointed Christ to be Head over everything in the Church, that the Church might be "the fulness of him," that is, complete in Him and filled with Him in every part.[10]

God's purpose to bring everything together in Christ was first seen as Christ's blood brought Jews and Gentiles together so that they became "one new man," one new body in Christ.[11] This, in the natural seemed an impossibility. The Jews looked on the Gentiles as dogs. The Gentiles scorned the Jews. That God could break down the barrier separating the two and actually "abolish" it, was a wonderful demonstration of God's ability to carry out His purpose.[12]

Paul keeps emphasizing this truth of the unity of Jews and Gentiles in Christ. This was the great mystery God gave him to reveal. His greatest joy was

---

[9] Galatians 4:4.
[10] Ephesians 1:23.
[11] Ephesians 2:13-16.
[12] Ephesians 2:15, 16; 3:10.

to preach the good news to the Gentiles that they were now part of the same body with the Jewish believer, heirs of the same promise.[13] He compares the Church further to one holy Temple into which each of us are being built "for an habitation of God through the Spirit."[14] The continuing accomplishment of this purpose will bring glory to God in and by the Church, in and by Christ (the body and the Head forever united) throughout all ages or generations "world without end" (an expression meaning "and for eternity").[15]

In addition to the evidence of what God is doing in the Church, believers have a personal guarantee that God will carry out His purpose. "After that ye believed, ye were sealed with that holy Spirit of promise."[16] "Promise" in the Greek is *"the* promise" and refers to "the promise of the Father," the baptism in the Holy Spirit.[17] "Sealing" in those days indicated identification, ownership, and approval. In this case it indicated that God has accepted our faith, marked us as His, and endued us with power from heaven.

The baptism in the Holy Spirit is also the "earnest of our inheritance until the redemption of the purchased possession."[18] "Earnest" means a first installment that is a sample and a guarantee of what is to come later. It is evidence of the redemption which has made us God's property. The day of our full redemption when we shall be changed is still future, but in the meantime, the Holy Spirit gives us the assurance that day will come.[19]

Ephesians, like all of Paul's epistles, has a practical

---

[13] Ephesians 3:2-9.
[14] Ephesians 2:22.
[15] Ephesians 3:21.
[16] Ephesians 1:13.

[17] Acts 1:4, 5; 2:4, 17, 18.
[18] Ephesians 1:14.
[19] Ephesians 4:30.

section. He begins it with an exhortation based on God's great purpose to bring everything together in one, in and by Christ. To share in God's purpose is a high calling. We must live in such a way as to be worthy of it, not that we can be worthy in ourselves, but we can make our lives correspond to our calling. We do this by maintaining attitudes of lowliness or humility free from any boasting, by meekness or gentleness with courtesy and consideration and longsuffering or forebearance and patience toward others, forebearing or putting up with one another in love, zealously making every effort to maintain "the unity of the Spirit in the bond of peace."[20] Why? Because God's purpose and our calling is one body, made one through the one Holy Spirit, kept one as we direct our hearts to the promise and hope of glory. This is made possible through the one Lord (Jesus), the one faith (the gospel), the one baptism (in view of Ephesians 1:13, 14; 4:30; this must mean the baptism in the Holy Spirit), and the One God and Father of all believers, who is over us all, works through us all, and dwells in us all.[21]

This recognition and application of God's eternal purpose is just as much needed today. The first century saw a demonstration of God's wisdom and power when in the Church He brought together in unity and peace Jews and Gentiles. In the Church He did what social agencies and men of good intentions in the world could not do. Surely, in these days when every effort to bring unity and peace in the world is failing, the world needs to see a similar demonstration. The blood of Jesus, the grace of God, and the power of the Spirit are still able to break

[20] Ephesians 4:3.   [21] Ephesians 4:1-6.

down barriers and bring people of different backgrounds into a new unity and fellowship with Christ as the Head. God will accomplish this when Jesus comes. But He wants to see it in His Church now!

Paul had God's purpose and our inheritance in the coming Kingdom in mind, too, when he went on to urge a love that would avoid all immorality, greediness, and the indecent acts, talks, and jokes or facetiousness of the world. Though not every place had the low morals of Corinth, the whole heathen world was rather indifferent to immorality, impurity, and greed. In fact, there were too many, even in the Church, who took a light attitude toward these things. But Paul warns against the power of their propaganda. He called them vain and empty words.[22] What do you think he would call the "new morality," or "situation ethics" today?

Christ as the Head of the Church, the Saviour of the Body, loved the Church and gave Himself for it to sanctify, consecrate, and cleanse it. Why? Because He wants to "present it to himself a glorious church, not having spot, or wrinkle, or any such thing; but that it should be holy and without blemish,"[23] members of His body, joined to Him as a Bride to a Husband. What greater encouragement to holiness could we have?

PRESENT AND FUTURE GOALS

Philippians 1:6 sets the theme for this epistle. God has begun a good work in the believers. He will continue to perform it until it is complete in the day of Jesus Christ, that is, at His Second Coming. He will then change our vile (weak, mortal) bodies,

---

[22] Ephesians 5:6.   [23] Ephesians 5:27, (25, 26, 30, 32).

making them like His glorious body through the power that enables Him to bring everything under subjection to His rule.[24]

This goal must affect all our choices. Those who make a god of physical desires or who make earthly things their goal prove by their lives that they are enemies of Christ. They will end up in the destruction of hell.[25] If we have the mind that was in Christ, we will humble ourselves as He did, recognizing that God "hath highly exalted him, and given him a name which is above every name."[26] The time is coming when every knee will bow and every tongue confess that Jesus Christ is Lord. So we humble ourselves now, make Him Lord now, begin to live as citizens of heaven now. We cannot center our attention on earthly things, because we wait so eagerly for our Saviour to come from heaven.[27]

In view of this goal, what Paul wanted most was to know the resurrection power of Christ in his life and service now, even if it meant sharing Christ's suffering and becoming like Him in His death.[28] His prayer for others also was that they too would choose the best. It would take a growth in love until love ceased being a mere impulse and became a guiding principle. It would take the knowledge of the Word and the judgment or wisdom of the Spirit. But it would mean that they would be sincere and pure in motives, without offense or blame in the day of Christ.

In view of the future goal we also have a present goal to work out our own salvation into our daily lives with fear and trembling, giving God the op-

---

[24] Philippians 3:21.
[25] Philippians 3:18, 19.
[26] Philippians 2:9.
[27] Philippians 3:20.
[28] Philippians 3:10.

portunity to be the Energizer, the Dynamic, bringing about His will in us. This means we will live and work without murmurings or grumbling, secret talk, or whispered complaints, and without arguing. That is, we will be more concerned about maintaining Christian fellowship and the unity of the Spirit than about our own feelings. Then we will be blameless and innocent of anything that might disrupt the body or give offense. The result will be that we can be effective witnesses, true to the "word of life" and shining as lights in the midst of a crooked or unscrupulous and perverse, perverted, misled, and depraved age.[29]

To sum it up, Philippians teaches that we must, if we are mature children of God, press toward the mark, run eagerly and steadily toward the goal, striving to win the prize—the upward call which God will give us in Christ when He comes.[30]

Treasure in Heaven

Colossians is very similar to Ephesians in many ways. Where Ephesians emphasizes the Church as the body of Christ, however, Colossians draws our attention to Christ as the Head. Where Ephesians points to what we will share as God works out His eternal purpose in the Church, Colossians shows us what is ours in Christ Himself.

The difference is chiefly in point of view. God's purpose is still the same as in Ephesians. He made peace through the blood of Christ's cross that in Christ He might reconcile everything to Himself. This has been demonstrated in us by the change that came when we were saved.[31] It will continue to be

[29] Philippians 2:12-16.
[30] Philippians 3:13-15.
[31] Colossians 1:20, 21.

demonstrated in us if we continue in the faith, grounded, established, settled, and steadfast, and if we do not permit ourselves to be moved or shifted from the hope which the gospel proclaims. Then, in the Day of Judgment, we will be presented holy, blameless, and irreproachable before Him.

Colossians also gives a great deal more attention to heaven than does Ephesians. That is because Christ is there. Though Christ is now in us, and this gives us a sure hope of sharing the glory to come, what we hope for is really kept safe for us in heaven.[32] There is a sense in which we are now in Christ's kingdom,[33] but Christ is still in heaven. We have been raised to new life in Christ. But Christ is really our life, so we set our hearts on Him and wait for the time when He will appear. Not until then will we appear with Him and share His glory and His throne.[34] Our joy and our thanks to God now are not merely for present blessings but for the fact that He has made us fit to be partakers of that inheritance which God has for His people.[35]

Someone has compared our position now to that of an underground army in a kingdom taken over by an enemy. Though their king might not be present with them, they are loyal to him. They are in communication with him. They are a part of his kingdom. When he returns and takes over again, they will be recognized for what they are and they will share in his victory. So now we belong to Christ, we are part of His kingdom, but His kingdom has not yet come on earth. Now we serve Him faithfully, but not until He comes will we share in His glory.

---

[32] Colossians 1:5, 27.
[33] Colossians 1:15; see John 3:3-5.
[34] Colossians 3:1-4.
[35] Colossians 1:12.

A Purifying Hope

We can include First John with these epistles of Paul, because when John looks toward the Second Coming in his First Epistle he sees the same truths and the same purifying hope. It recognizes that though we belong to God, the present world is under the rule of the Evil One.[36] It recognizes also that though we are now children of God, it is not yet apparent, not yet revealed what we shall be. But we know that when Christ appears we shall be like Him, for we shall see Him as He really is. It is this hope within us that encourages us to keep ourselves pure, just as Christ is pure. This means we will not keep on sinning the same old sins.[37] We will do what is right. We will not close our hearts to a brother in need.[38] We will also watch out for false doctrines and cults that have a false view of Christ and show the spirit of Antichrist. The Antichrist is coming, but we must not put the danger off into the future. The same spirit that will trap men when he is made manifest is already present in the world. But we need not fear if we walk in love and if we live our lives in the fear of God and for Christ.

---

[36] 1 John 5:19.   [38] 1 John 3:17.
[37] 1 John 3:6.

Questions

1. How does the Book of Galatians guard against misusing our Christian freedom?

2. What guarantee do we have that God will carry out His great purpose for the Church?

3. What will help us attain the goal God has for us? What will keep us from it?

4. Why does the Book of Colossians focus our attention on heaven?

5. What are the things that these epistles encourage us to do and not do in the light of Christ's coming?

8 Caught Up to Meet Him

WAITING FOR CHRIST TO COME

Paul gives more attention to the Second Coming in his letters to the Thessalonians than in any of his other epistles. Paul went to Thessalonica teaching from the Scriptures that Christ must suffer and rise again, showing them that the resurrection of Jesus proves He is the Christ.[1] The result was a mighty move of God that brought the conversion of a great multitude. It also so stirred unbelievers that they cried out, "These that have turned the world upside down are come hither also."[2]

This mighty move of God raised the Thessalonian believers to a high level of faith and expectancy. Because the gospel came to them not "in word only, but also in power, and in the Holy Ghost, and in much assurance,"[3] they followed Paul and the Lord in spite of persecution, "with joy of the Holy Ghost."[4] This revival spirit continued, and the news of their vibrant faith spread in all directions, stirring the other young churches in Greece and Macedonia. The Thessalonians became a wonderful example to them of people who had turned away from idols to serve and obey the true and living God and to wait with expectancy for His Son to come from heaven. They believed Jesus died and rose again. Now they were thrilled with

[1] Acts 17:2, 3.
[2] Acts 17:6.
[3] 1 Thessalonians 1:5.
[4] 1 Thessalonians 1:6.

the thought of what that would mean for them when He comes. How wonderful it would be to share God's own kingdom and God's glory with Him.[5]

READY FOR CHRIST TO COME

Paul did more than commend the Thessalonians for their hope of Christ's coming. It was important for them to have that hope. It was more important to be ready. Paul, in his preaching and teaching in Thessalonica, had already given them information about the "times and seasons."[6] That is, he told them about the warnings and instructions Jesus gave. They understood that the Father did not intend for them to know the times or seasons.[7] They knew very well that the Day of the Lord would come as a thief in the night. They knew that when that day came people would be talking about peace and safety. Then sudden destruction would come on them. They would not be able to avoid or run away from this any more than a woman with child could avoid or run away from birth pangs.[8]

Does this mean the Christian has to be taken by surprise when Jesus comes? It may be that many will be. Too many today have come to feel that the only thing important about the Second Coming is the time and the order of events. Because these things are so controversial, many are confused. Some feel that there is nothing they can know for sure about our Lord's coming. Some, to avoid controversy, neglect the subject almost altogether. Some even join the scoffers who follow their own desires and who say, "Where is the promise of his coming?"[9] They claim

---

[5] 1 Thessalonians 2:12.
[6] 1 Thessalonians 5:1.
[7] Acts 1:7.

[8] 1 Thessalonians 5:2-4.
[9] 2 Peter 3:4.

tnat this world will continue on indefinitely. But Peter points out that they willfully ignore that God did bring an end once—in the Flood. The reason for the delay in Christ's coming is not procrastination on God's part. He does not look at time as we do. He is also very concerned to give further opportunity for men to come to repentance. But this does not mean He will put it off forever. "The day of the Lord will come," says Peter.[10] Peter also reminds us that it will take men by surprise, "as a thief in the night."

But Christians do not need to be taken by surprise. His coming does not need to be like that of a thief in the night for us. It is the world that is in the night of ignorance and unbelief. But we are not in darkness, nor do we belong to the darkness. We are children of light, for the light of Christ and the gospel has flooded our hearts and minds. We are children of the day. This means even more. We are heirs of the blessings and glory of that day when our Lord will be revealed from heaven. We have a knowledge and a hope that will help us to be ready even though we do not and cannot know exactly when Jesus will return.

What part do we have then? How can we be sure that that day does not take us by surprise so that we miss the glory? First, we must begin to act as if we belong to the light and to that day. This means keeping wide awake, on the alert, and spiritually sober. The sober person avoids anything that would produce in his spirit the results that drunkenness produces in the body and mind. The Greek word means well balanced, self-controlled, and free from excesses, rash-

---

[10] 2 Peter 3:10.

ness, and confusion. We show soberness when we face the battle for the Lord wearing faith and love as a breastplate (body armor) and our hope of salvation as a helmet.[11] Only this kind of life is worthy of the glory and the kingdom God has prepared for us.

Then, notice how Paul connects faith and love with our hope. Paul's prayer was that God might let him come and complete what was lacking in the faith of the Thessalonians.[12] Since "faith cometh by hearing, and hearing by the Word of God,"[13] we may be sure Paul meant to give them teaching that would supply what they needed.

Thirdly, Paul's prayer also was that the Lord would make them increase and abound or overflow in love. This was just as necessary as a well-grounded faith, for love is the essence, the climax, and the summation of the obedience God wants, of the fruit of the Spirit, and of the Christian walk.[14] By the strengthening of their faith and knowledge of the Word, and by the continued growth and overflow of their love, God will "stablish" or confirm and strengthen our hearts so that we can stand before God blameless in holiness when Jesus comes "with all his saints."[15] If we would be ready for Jesus to come then, the most important thing is to study the Scriptures and seek God for greater love. If we do this, He will see to it that we are ready. He will be faithful to complete the work of sanctification (or consecration) which was begun when we first dedicated our lives to God. He will keep us body, soul, mind, and spirit, so that we will be blameless in the day Jesus comes.[16]

---

[11] 1 Thessalonians 5:8, 9.
[12] 1 Thessalonians 3:10.
[13] Romans 10:17.
[14] Matthew 22:37-39; James 2:8; Galatians 5:14; 2 Peter 1:3-8.
[15] 1 Thessalonians 3:13.
[16] 1 Thessalonians 5:23.

At the risk of digressing, it might be worth mentioning a controversial area here. Bible scholars disagree about the meaning of the phrase "with all his saints." Some identify it with Zechariah 14:5, where the Lord returns at the end of the Great Tribulation to the Mount of Olives. Others point out that "saints" or "holy ones" often means angels. Deuteronomy 33: 2 says that at Sinai the Lord came with ten thousand of His saints to give them the Law. The New Testament understands these saints to be angels. Acts 7:53 speaks of the Law received by the disposition of angels. Galatians 3:19 speaks of the Law being ordained by angels. Hebrews 2:2 calls the Law the word spoken by angels. This is in accord with Mark 8:38, where Jesus says that when He comes in the glory of His Father with the holy angels, He will be ashamed of those who are now ashamed of Him and of His words. Matthew 25:31 records that the Son of man and the holy angels will come in His glory and he will sit upon His throne.

There are other possibilities. "With his saints" may mean simply "in the midst of His saints." That is, when He returns it will be to be in the midst of His saints. Or, the phrase may refer to the Thessalonians instead of to Christ's coming. Paul may mean that God would stablish or strengthen their hearts that along with all his saints they might be blameless in holiness at Christ's coming. Since Paul goes on to talk about a coming where all believers, both living and dead, rise to meet Jesus, we must take this latter view or else consider the "saints" or "holy ones" in this verse to be angels.

RISING TO MEET HIM

The reason Paul discusses the subject of the resurrection of the dead seems to be that false teachers were telling the Thessalonians that they would miss something if they were not alive when Jesus returned. Some believers had already died. Was there something wrong with their faith? Would they remain as disembodied spirits in heaven and fail to receive the new body God has for us? Would they be left behind and miss out in the glory to be revealed when Jesus returns? Would only the living share in the joys of the Kingdom?

If this were so we might have reason to grieve with almost the same hopeless sorrow of the heathen. But we have a better hope than that. Jesus died and rose again. "Even so them also which sleep in Jesus will God bring with him."[17] "In Jesus" is not the ordinary phrase here. It is literally "through Jesus," or "by the agency of Jesus." "With" is also a different word from that of 1 Thessalonians 3:13 It means identification or union and speaks of the Resurrection. The meaning, then, is that by the agency of Jesus, God will bring back the dead through the Resurrection, a resurrection made possible because they belong to Christ.

Paul goes on to say that those who are still alive when Jesus comes will not "prevent" those who are already dead. "Prevent" is used here in its old English sense of "get ahead of" or "precede." Those who are still alive will not have any advantage whatsoever. In fact, when Jesus comes there will be the shout of command, the voice of the archangel, and

[17] 1 Thessalonians 4:14.

the sound of God's trumpet (these taking place in heaven as all heaven hears the signal that God's time has come). Then Jesus will descend from heaven and the dead in Christ (those who were "in Christ," with Christ as the center of their lives at the time of their death) will rise first. Then those believers who are still alive will be caught up, snatched up, together with them and at exactly the same time.[18] Thus, it will not matter whether we live or die. We will be united then, as we rise in the clouds to meet Jesus. None of us will miss anything of that glorious experience.

This sudden snatching away to meet Jesus is what is often called the Rapture. Some people today belittle this word. But it is a legitimate expression. The Latin word used to translate the catching or snatching away is the root of our words rapt and rapture. Today, these words are used in English to mean spiritual or emotional ecstasy. But even in English the older meaning of the words are to be lifted and transported to another place by supernatural power. A power greater than gravity, greater than the mighty rockets that lift our astronauts, will lift us just as Jesus was lifted in His ascension.

"To meet the Lord" is another unusual expression. Literally, it is "for a meeting with the Lord." The Greek word translated "meeting" is a special word often used in connection with the coming (Greek, *parousia*) of a king or governor to visit a city. In those days the citizens would go out to meet such a person and then would escort him on the last part of his journey into the city. Christians often did this

---

[18] 1 Thessalonians 4:15-17.

when one of their leaders was coming. Even when
Paul was being brought as a prisoner to Rome, as
soon as the Roman believers heard he was in Italy,
they walked thirty-nine miles down the Appian Way
to meet him and escort him into the city.[19] Jesus
used the same phraseology of the virgins going to
meet the bridegroom.[20]

Paul does not say anything directly at this point
concerning our escorting the Lord back to earth after
we meet Him in the air. His only emphasis is "so
shall we ever be with the Lord"[21] This is what Paul
longed for. More than heaven itself he wanted to be
with Jesus. He could think of no greater comfort or
encouragement for the Thessalonian believers. Christ
died for us that whether we live or die we shall live
together with Him when He comes. This is the reason
why all Christians ought to encourage, help, and edify
one another.[22]

RESCUED FROM THE WRATH TO COME

Paul did have another reason for encouraging believers to be faithful and to watch and pray. If they
should be ready when Jesus comes they would be a
source of joy for Him then.[23] This implies that Paul
expected Christ to review the work of His servants
in the manner that Jesus described in the parables
of the talents and the pounds.[24] It indicates also that
the first thing that will happen when we rise to meet
Jesus in the air will be the judgment seat of Christ.

At this time Paul hoped to be among those who
would still be alive and would rise to meet Jesus and
receive their crown and reward.[25] Later, when he

---

[19] Acts 28:15.
[20] Matthew 25:6.
[21] 1 Thessalonians 4:17.
[22] 1 Thessalonians 5:10, 11.

[23] 1 Thessalonians 2:19.
[24] Matthew 25:14-30; Luke 19:11-27
[25] 1 Thessalonians 2:19; 4:17.

wrote to the Corinthians, he included himself with those who will rise from the dead.[26] Perhaps this was because he knew he did not know the times or the seasons. But the time came when he knew he was soon to die as a martyr. He was not in the least disappointed then that he would not live until the Rapture. He was ready for his life to be poured out as an offering before the Lord. He had fought, not merely *a* good fight, but *the* good fight, the only fight worth fighting. His work was behind him now. But he did not think of death as before him. The thing that was before him was "a crown of righteousness, which the Lord, the righteous judge, shall give me at that day: and not to me only, but unto all them also that love his appearing."[27]

Thank God for this promise of a crown and rewards at the judgment seat of Christ. We too can rejoice there if we truly love His appearing. By loving His appearing, however, the Bible does not mean merely that we love to hear about it, talk about it, think about, or sing about it. There is more than one word for love in the Greek. The one used here is a high, holy, self-giving love that is utterly and completely loyal. We must love His appearing in this way. Are we living so that the judgment seat of Christ will be just another opportunity for us to express our love and loyalty to Him? Then, for us, as for Paul, it will be a wonderful day.

Paul's attitude here shows that he is not looking for any general judgment of both righteous and wicked at the same time. He knows he will appear before the judgment seat of Christ, but that has nothing to do with the wrath and judgment which will come on the

[26] 1 Corinthians 6:14; 2 Corinthians 4:14.   [27] 2 Timothy 4:8.

world and on the wicked. In fact, one of the reasons we wait so expectantly for Christ to come from heaven is because He is our Preserver, Deliverer, or Rescuer "from the wrath to come."[28] Some Bible scholars argue about the prepositions here, but they overlook Romans 5:9. The clear meaning is that by snatching us away in the Rapture, Jesus will preserve us from the wrath which will then fall on the earth.

This is even more emphatic in 1 Thessalonians 5:9. We keep awake spiritually and we live sober, well-balanced, self-controlled lives, wearing the gospel armor of faith, love, and the hope of salvation because God has a future salvation or deliverance for us. He has not appointed us to wrath. Instead of suffering God's wrath, we shall be caught away and live together with Him. He will not wait to rescue us after the wrath is fallen and we suffer for a while. We are not destined for wrath at all.

Wrath is the kind of anger and indignation that any judge should feel against sin and evil. God, as the Judge of all, feels wrath against the evil that is ruining the world for which Christ died. Because He loves mankind He hates the sin that destroys them. The Bible in both Old and New Testaments declares again and again that God will pour out His wrath—that is, wrathful judgment—on sin and evil. There will be a day of wrath which will reveal the righteous judgment of God on impenititent, disobedient hearts.[29]

That wrath will begin when the judgments of God fall on the earth at the end of this age during what is called the Great Tribulation. The Bible clearly

---

[28] 1 Thessalonians 1:10.   [29] Romans 2:5; Ephesians 5:6; Colossians 3:6.

calls these judgments the wrath of God.[30] They are so stated that no one could be anywhere on earth, not even in some backwoods cave, and escape their effects. This is one of the strongest arguments for believing that the Church will not go through the Great Tribulation. We are not appointed unto wrath.

A few years ago a man distributed what he labeled as "One Hundred Reasons Why the Church Will Go Through the Tribulation." Careful examination showed that his hundred reasons boiled down to one —God has not promised that the Church would escape tribulation and suffering. The point he missed is that when the Bible talks about tribulation it talks about two different things. Sometimes the word refers to the distress, persecution, trouble, pressure, and anguish of heart that outward circumstances may bring upon a Christian as he serves the Lord in a godless world. The same Greek word translated "tribulation" is translated "affliction" when Paul talks about our light or slight affliction, which in the light of eternity is but for a moment, and which "worketh for us a far more exceeding and eternal weight of glory."[31] But the judgments of the Great Tribulation are not in the same class. They are God's wrath. Any interpretation of the Book of Revelation must take this fact into account.

The comfort and encouragement that Paul gives in First Thessalonians, then, is based on the wonderful hope that whether we are alive or dead when Jesus comes, we will be caught up to meet Him among the clouds in the air. The exhortations He gives are based on the need to live in such a way so as to show that

---

[30] Revelation 15:1; 16:1.   [31] 2 Corinthians 4:17.

we really have this hope and that we really want to be ready. Paul pictures our life as one of joy and rejoicing now that will bring even greater joy and rejoicing when Jesus comes.

QUESTIONS

1. Why was the hope of the Lord's coming so wonderful and real to the Thessalonians?

2. What should keep the Christian from being taken by surprise when Jesus comes?

3. What does it mean for the believer to watch and be sober?

4. What is necessary on our part if God is to establish or strengthen and confirm our hearts?

5. Why were the Thessalonians disturbed about the fact that some Christians there had died?

6. What is meant by the "Rapture"?

7. What assurance can we draw from First Thessalonians that the Church will not go through the Tribulation?

9 The Brightness of His Coming

2 THESSALONIANS

COMING WITH FLAMING FIRE

Apparently, what Paul wrote in 1 Thessalonians raised even more questions about the Second Coming. The Thessalonian believers were suffering a great deal of persecution. How long would they have to suffer? What would happen to their persecutors?

Paul answers them in 2 Thessalonians. First, he commends their faith and patient endurance. Then he points them to a time "when the Lord Jesus shall be revealed from heaven,"[1] literally, to the apocalypse or disclosure or revealing of the Lord Jesus. Then, those who are now suffering trouble, tribulation, or pressure, will be in a state of rest or relief, free from toil and conflict. Those persecutors, however, along with all who reject the knowledge of God or who do not obey the gospel, will be judged by a just God and punished with flaming fire. They will suffer eternal destruction, cut off forever from the presence of the Lord, never to share the glory, splendor, radiance, and royal magnificence of His power and might. In contrast to this, at His coming Jesus will be glorified and honored among His saints (the believers, because the Thessalonians are included among them). He will also be admired or marveled at by all who

[1] 2 Thessalonians 1:7.

believe. That is, they will marvel as they see the revelation of His supernatural power and glory in His coming and in the judgment of His enemies.

The word "apocalypse" used in 2 Thessalonians 1:7 is often used of the revelation of truth as in Romans 16:25 and Ephesians 1:17. It always implies truth not only revealed but made clear and understood.[2] This is the reason for the marveling of those who believe.[3] Not until they actually see the supernatural power of Jesus as He takes vengeance (the Greek means to give out just punishment) with flaming fire will they fully understand what this means.

This passage has nothing to do with the appearance of Christ to catch away the believers as discussed in 1 Thessalonians 4:17. There, the emphasis is on what will happen to us as we rise into the air to meet the Lord and be with Him. Here, the emphasis is on what will happen to unbelievers when Christ returns with the fire of judgment. Here the believers are already relaxed and at rest, already free from their toil and conflict as they stand by and watch the revelation of divine judgment. In 2 Thessalonians 2:1, Paul does speak again of the coming (*parousia*) of Christ and "our gathering together unto him." This is more literally, "Now in contrast to what we have just been talking about in chapter one, we request of you, brothers, with reference to the coming *parousia,* the first stage of the return of our Lord Jesus Christ even our assembling with Him." Clearly, Paul indicates that he is leaving the subject which was dealt with in the first chapter and going back to what he

---

[2] Ephesians 1:18.   [3] 2 Thessalonians 1:10.

had already written them about in 1 Thessalonians 4:17.

The revelation of Christ with his mighty, supernatural angels will then correspond to our escorting or accompanying Christ back to earth after meeting Him in the air, as we have pointed out what the word "meeting" implies. Paul does not say here how long it will be between Christ's coming for us and this return with us, but as 1 Thessalonians 2:19 indicated, Paul expected rewards at the judgment seat of Christ, and here we see the Christians already rewarded, and giving honor and glory to Christ.

Paul also goes on to mention the final judgment of eternal destruction.[4] This is the judgment of the great white throne. We must recognize, therefore, that Paul is more concerned about the fact of judgment than about distinguishing between the various judgments. It was not until a number of years later that God gave John on the Isle of Patmos the revelation that a thousand years would come between the judgment seat of Christ and the great white throne. Paul had already told the Thessalonians that he was concerned about the fact of Christ's coming and the necessity of being ready lest it take them by surprise like a thief in the night. Now he is emphasizing the fact that their persecutors will be punished, so he includes both the judgment that will come when Christ returns with His saints and angels, and the final separation that will be their ultimate destiny.

THE COMING OF THE "FALLING AWAY"

The purpose of the second chapter of 2 Thessalonians was to correct another false teaching about

---

[4] 2 Thessalonians 1:9.

the Second Coming. Some of Paul's enemies were spreading their doctrine, even writing letters in Paul's name and forging his signature to them. They taught that Paul was wrong in saying that the first stage of our Lord's coming was a resurrection and a snatching away to meet Christ in the air. In fact, they said the "day of Christ," that is, the time of His return for rewards and punishments, was "at hand."[5] The phrase "at hand" is translated "present" when Paul talks about "this present evil world" or age.[6] The Greek means that these false teachers claimed the Day of Christ had already come and was still present. It had begun and was already going on. It may be that these false teachers also claimed that Christ had already returned, spiritually, or in some other way. Some false cults today still teach that we cannot expect a literal return of Christ. Some even say we are in the Millennium already.

Paul denies this as emphatically as possible. "Let no man deceive you by any means: for that day shall not come, except there come a falling away first, and that man of sin be revealed, the son of perdition."[7] The words "that day shall not come" are supplied by the King James translators, but they are necessary for the sense, as the preceding verse clearly indicates. "A falling away" is literally "the apostasy," or "the rebellion," that is, the great rebellion, which here seems to be closely connected with the man of sin being revealed or disclosed.

Just what "the falling away" is, is another matter of controversy. Some take it as a religious apostasy. The Greek word also means a forsaking, an abandon-

---

[5] 2 Thessalonians 2:2.   [7] 2 Thessalonians 2:3.
[6] Galatians 1:4.

ment (as in Acts 21:21, where it is used of forsaking or abandoning the Law of Moses). This interpretation indicates that the thing which gives the Antichrist an opportunity to take over is a great abandonment of spiritual religion. Other Bible scholars object to this, saying that we have had many times of religious apostasy in the history of the Church. One writer asks how anything could be worse than the terrible apostasy which preceded the great Reformation under Martin Luther. Perhaps if that writer would look around in the world today he would have his answer.

Nevertheless, some do take the falling away or apostasy in its more common meaning of rebellion. They say that a great world war dominated by godless rebels will provide the opportunity for the man of sin to be revealed and take over. In view of the seals of Revelation 6 which indicate war, conquest, famine, and death, there may be some grounds for this interpretation. Certainly the world today seems headed for that kind of world revolution.

Another point of controversy is the meaning of the word "first" in 2 Thessalonians 2:3. Some take it to mean that the apostasy and the man of sin must come first before the Lord comes to snatch away the believers to meet the Lord in the air. This interpretation claims that Paul means that these things are signs preceding the Rapture, and that therefore the Church will go through the Great Tribulation. The most common meaning of the word "first," however, is first in a sequence. That is, the first thing after the Day of the Lord begins will be the falling away and the revelation of the man of sin.

The whole point of Paul's words of exhortation here seems to be that the Thessalonians were being shaken from the hope that the Lord would come and gather them to meet Him. If they were already in the Day of Christ and everything was taking place on earth, then there would be no catching away. But Paul says this is a deception. If they were left behind on earth and the Day of the Lord was already in progress, the first thing that would happen would be this great apostasy and the disclosure of the man of sin. Since this had not happened, the false teachers were wrong and the Thessalonian believers could continue looking forward to the Rapture.

THE COMING OF THE ANTICHRIST

Paul shows also that the man of sin will continue for some time—long enough to set himself up against everything divine, against every object of worship, and to take over in God's temple and claim to be God.[8] His coming, or rather, his presence will be energized by Satan's power with all kinds of miracles, signs, and false wonders.[9] But all this will come to an end when Jesus returns and slays him with the breath of His mouth (the same Greek word means both breath and spirit) and puts an end to him "with the brightness of his coming."[10] The brightness of His coming is more literally the appearing or visible manifestation (*epiphaneia*) of His coming (*parousia*). It corresponds to the coming with flaming fire and to the coming of Christ as the Word of God and as King of kings and Lord of lords.[11] Then, His word becomes a sword of the Spirit in His mouth, as Paul says in 2 Thessalonians 2:8. There is no place for the catching away of the saints in this picture, either.

---

[8] 2 Thessalonians 2:4.
[9] 2 Thessalonians 2:9
[10] 2 Thessalonians 2:8.

[11] 2 Thessalonians 1:8;
Revelation 19:11-17.

Clearly, the saints are not on earth during the Antichrist's rule, but are caught away before he is revealed.

The term "antichrist" comes from 1 John. John names him and recognizes that the people had been taught about him, but gives no details.[12] John's purpose was to remind them that the spirit of antichrist is already in the world, and that this, not the future Antichrist, is our primary concern now. Paul recognized the same thing when he said, "the mystery of iniquity doth already work."[13] "Iniquity" here is lawlessness. It is the same word translated "sin" in verse 3 and "wicked" in verse 8.[14] But this does not mean that present lawlessness is the complete fulfillment of what the Bible teaches here, as some today try to say. There is something holding back the revelation of the Antichrist now. Paul had already explained what this was in his preaching and teaching at Thessalonica. But he does not explain it here. This has resulted in all kinds of speculation as to what the hindrance and the hinderer are.

It is clear that "what withholdeth" or "holds back" in 2 Thessalonians 2:6 is neuter gender in the Greek. "He who now letteth," in verse 7, is the same Greek word in the masculine. Many interpreters, both ancient and modern, took verse 6 to refer to the Roman Empire, and verse 7 to refer to the emperor. Other ancient interpreters took verse 6 to refer to the preaching of the apostles, and verse 7 to the Apostle Paul. But these interpretations do not account for the fact that the Antichrist has not yet been revealed.

Another interpretation recognizes that the word

---

[12] 1 John 2:18.
[13] 2 Thessalonians 2:7.
[14] See 1 Timothy 1:9 where the plural of the same word is translated "the lawless."

"spirit" in the Greek is neuter, and the Greek usually uses neuter pronouns to refer even to the Holy Spirit, as in Romans 8:16. Thus the power which holds back the revelation of the Antichrist could very well be the Holy Spirit. But it is not the Holy Spirit who is taken out of the way so that the Antichrist can be disclosed and begin his work. Now, if we recognize that the Holy Spirit works through the individual believer in this age, the masculine word of verse 7 could very well refer to the believer, and indicate that he must be taken out of the way. This fits in with all these other facts which indicate that the Rapture will take place before the Antichrist is revealed. We look for Christ, not for the Antichrist.

The Antichrist is also called the "son of perdition." This is a phrase meaning one who is doomed to destruction or eternal loss. The same phrase is used of Judas Iscariot,[15] for he had the same doom. Paul goes on to say that those who are deceived by the Antichrist all will share his doom. In fact, they are called "them that perish," or who are doomed to destruction and eternal loss. They are deceived because "they received not the love of the truth, that they might be saved."[16] "Saved" here does not mean converted. It refers to the salvation to which the Christians are now looking forward, the salvation which will be accomplished when we are changed as we are caught away to meet the Lord.[17] In this same passage,[18] Paul gives thanks that, in contrast to those deceived by the Antichrist, God has chosen that our end would be salvation and the obtaining of the glory of our Lord Jesus Christ. Verse 10, then, refers to

---

[15] John 17:21.
[16] 2 Thessalonians 2:10.

[17] Romans 13:11; 1 Thessalonians 5:9.
[18] 2 Thessalonians 2:13, 14.

those who have already missed that salvation. That is, they have been left behind after the Rapture. Part of their judgment will be the strong deluding influence which will cause them to believe a lie (literally, *the* lie, the pretensions of the Antichrist), thus assuring their final judgment.[19]

COMING TO BRING A NEW HEAVENS
AND A NEW EARTH

Paul has only a little to say about the final judgment. He focuses most of his attention on what will happen at the end of this age. The revelation of Christ's glory and the doom of the Antichrist should be enough to make us want to live in readiness for Jesus to come. But Peter in his second epistle jumps over those events, even past the great white throne, and focuses our attention on what will happen at the end of the "day of the Lord."[20] During that day (not before it) the heavens will pass away, come to an end, or disappear with a great noise (like the roar of a tremendous fire), and the elements (the heavenly bodies, the sun, moon, and stars) will melt or be destroyed with fervent or consuming heat. The earth also with all the works or accomplishments of men that we now see in it will be burned up, or as one ancient version found in Egypt puts it, will disappear (so that it cannot be found).

Some today try to apply this to the renovation of the earth which must take place in order to bring in the glorious conditions of the Millennium. They point out that the word translated "melt" in verse 10 is sometimes used of untying bonds or fetters,

---

[19] 2 Thessalonians 2:12.   [20] 2 Peter 3:10.

unloosing sandal thongs, releasing prisoners, and even
of a woman loosing down her hair. It also means
to break up into component parts, and is used of
tearing down a house or of a ship breaking up on the
rocks. But it is also used of destroying, bringing to
an end, abolishing, and doing away with altogether.

The mention here of the heavens disappearing and
the elements or heavenly bodies being destroyed by
heat does not fit the beginning of the Millennium,
however. It does fit Isaiah 34:4, where the host of
heaven (the planets and stars) will be dissolved or
go to nothing like something that has rotted away and
the heavens will be rolled up like a scroll. We might
get the effect if we pull down a windowshade and
let it go quickly. With a "whoosh" the heavens will
be gone. It also fits Isaiah 51:6, which indicates that
heavens will vanish away like smoke and the earth
will be like an old garment that has rotted away and
falls apart into nothing. It fits Isaiah 65:17, "Behold,
I create a new heavens and a new earth: and the
former shall not be remembered, nor come into mind."
(Isaiah 65:20-25 goes back to millennial times because
Isaiah is also interested in the restoration of the
present Jerusalem according to God's promise.) This
new heaven and new earth, which God has not made
yet, will remain.[21]

Some interpreters object to this complete destruction of the present heavens and earth on the basis of
Psalms 93:1; 96:10; 104:5. But these passages have to
do with the relative stability of the earth in contrast
to other things. We must understand what these psalms
say in the light of Psalm 102:25-27, which indicates

---

[21] Isaiah 66:22.

that only God is eternal. The psalmist here compares what will happen to the heavens and earth to what happens when someone changes clothes. That is, you put off the old and put on something new and different. So God will replace the present heavens and earth with a brand new heavens and earth that are completely different. This is certainly the meaning of 2 Peter 3:13 and Revelation 21:1. It is a completely new creation, and everything in it will be brand new, not merely renovated or reconditioned.[22] The very substance will be new. John, for example, speaks of gold transparent like glass.[23] We do not know any transparent gold. We can pound out gold until it is only a few molecules thick and put it on a window as gold leaf, but the gold leaf is not transparent. John is just using human words to describe something that is completely different from anything we know in this present creation.

The old chemistry and physics which some of us learned in school did not leave room for this kind of destruction and new creation. But now that we have seen atomic material changed into energy in atomic reactions, what Peter described does not seem so impossible. The disintegration of matter does take place with consuming heat, just as Peter said. The discovery of antimatter also opens up the way to seeing a possibility of how this could be fulfilled. Positrons, antiprotons, and other antiparticles are produced in atomic reactions. When a positron meets an electron or when an antiproton meets a proton they annihilate each other. There is just a flash of energy (heat) and then nothing, for the heat energy goes off into

---

[22] Revelation 21:5.   [23] Revelation 21:21.

space. In these reactions ordinary particles and anti-particles are always produced in pairs. Some have suggested that this may mean that there is a universe of antimatter off somewhere, to correspond to the universe of matter we are familiar with. All God would have to do would be to let this universe of antimatter drift across our universe and with a great noise and fervent heat it would all be gone.

The universe of antimatter is, of course, speculation. But the new heavens and the new earth are not. They are God's promise. May we live and teach with that promise in view.

QUESTIONS

1. What encouragement does Paul give to help the Thessalonians endure their persecutions?

2. What is the relation of Christ's coming with fire to Christ's coming to catch away the believers?

3. What is the nature of the Antichrist and when will he be revealed?

4. What does Paul say in this chapter about the final judgment?

5. What does Peter say about the end of this present heaven and earth? How will it take place?

6. What indicates that the new heavens and earth will be brand new?

10 The Cross and The Crown

WE SHALL REIGN

Paul's letters to Timothy and Titus are full of practical advice to help these young men with the ministry of the Word and the supervision of the churches. But dominating everything is the eager expectation of "that blessed hope, and the glorious appearing of the great God and our Saviour Jesus Christ."[1] To Paul that "blessed hope" meant the fulfillment of God's purpose and calling.[2] It included the full expression of eternal life, an immortal body, eternal glory, and a crown.[3]

Along with this hope, Paul urged Timothy to remind his hearers of something else. Because Paul wanted the Christians to obtain the salvation which is in Christ Jesus along with eternal glory, he endured everything, bearing hardship patiently, even being chained as a criminal. He went on to say, "It is a faithful saying: For if we be dead with him, we shall also live with him: If we suffer, we shall also reign with him: if we deny him, he also will deny us: If we believe not, yet he abideth faithful: he cannot deny himself."[4]

The word "suffer" in verse 12 is the same as the word translated "endure" in verse 10. It has the meaning of standing one's ground, holding out, bearing up against difficulties. It means staying in the

---

[1] Titus 2:13.
[2] 2 Timothy 1:9.
[3] 2 Timothy 1:10; 2:10; 4:8.
[4] 2 Timothy 2:11-13.

battle when others are deserting, staying in the race when others are dropping out, going on and going through, regardless of what others do. Only if we continue to endure will we reign as kings with Jesus. If we deny or turn away from Him, He will deny us. If we are unfaithful ("believe not" is a phrase used of disloyal soldiers), this does not mean God will be unfaithful to His plan. He will find someone. He will find some way. He cannot be untrue to Himself.

If we are to reign with Christ, then, it is absolutely necessary to be true to Jesus to the end. Paul always had the same thing in mind when he compared the Christian life to an athletic contest. Athletes put themselves under strict training rules, exercising self-control and disciplining themselves because they wanted to win a victor's crown, actually a wreath made of leaves.[5] They went into the race with the realization that it was possible to lose, so they put everything they had into it.

There is a crown waiting for each one of us, a far more wonderful crown than the crown of leaves, which would soon wither.[6] But we cannot have it by taking things easy or by living to please ourselves. It will take right motives, right methods, and right goals.[7] We can never win if we run uncertainly or aimlessly. Or, to change the illustration, we cannot win a boxing match by wasting our punches and beating the air.[8] How foolish it is to waste time and effort on things that do not count!

Paul, great apostle though he was, knew that he too needed to discipline himself. He disciplined his body and kept it under control. He refused to let

---

[5] 1 Corinthians 9:25.
[6] 2 Timothy 4:8.
[7] 2 Timothy 2:5.
[8] 2 Corinthians 9:26.

himself become a slave to his physical appetites and desires. His purpose was to make his body an instrument to do the will of God, to spread the gospel, to win the battle for the Lord. He knew that if he did not keep his body under control, the passions of the body could dominate again and make him a castaway.[9] "Castaway" is translated "reprobate" in Romans 1:28. A castaway is "filled with all unrighteousness, fornication, wickedness, covetousness," and a whole list of other sins.[10] The word's root meaning is "rejected after testing." It was used of dross that had no gold or silver in it and was fit for nothing but to be thrown on the slag heap. Paul was determined by the grace of God and the help of the Holy Spirit to let nothing keep him from winning the crown.

James also saw the need of continuing faithful under testing in order to "receive the crown of life, which the Lord hath promised to them that love him."[11] Paul adds that the man belonging to God must flee from, or guard against, such traps as the love of money and energetically pursue righteousness, godliness, faith, love, endurance, and gentleness. At the same time he must fight the good fight of faith and take firm hold on eternal life, "until the appearing of our Lord Jesus Christ."[12]

Paul himself lived this way. When he finally faced death, he was able to say, "I have fought a good fight, I have finished my course, I have kept the faith."[13] He had stayed in the battle. He had run the race to the finish line. He knew the crown was waiting.

[9] 1 Corinthians 9:27.
[10] Romans 1:29-32.
[11] James 1:12.
[12] 1 Timothy 6:10-14; Titus 2:12, 13.
[13] 2 Timothy 4:7.

CREATED TO REIGN

The crown that God has for us was not an after-thought on His part. He did not raise Jesus from the dead, exalt Him to the heavenly throne, and then suddenly decide that it would be nice to let us reign with Him. The crown was part of God's original purpose for man when He first said, "Let us make man in our image."[14] God's nature and character do not change. Neither does His faithfulness to His purpose and His promises.

The Book of Hebrews brings out the fact that we do not see the fullness of God's image in man now. But we do see it in Christ. Neither do we see man ruling now, but we do see Christ.[15]

To bring this out, Hebrews quotes Psalm 8:4-6. "What is man, that thou art mindful of him? or the son of man, that thou visitest him? Thou madest him a little lower [or, for a little time lower] than the angels; thou crownedst him with glory and honour, and didst set him over the works of thy hands: thou hast put all things in subjection under his feet."[16]

The psalmist was looking back to the first chapter of Genesis. That chapter emphasizes that man was the climax of all God's creation. Only man was created in the image and likeness of God. This seems to imply three things. (1) Man was created a spiritual being, with a spiritual nature capable of fellowship and communion with God, who is Spirit. (2) Man was created a moral being, capable of choice, capable of reflecting the holiness and righteousness of God. (3) Man was meant to share in God's work of ruling His universe.

---

[14] Genesis 1:26.
[15] Hebrews 1:3.

[16] Hebrews 2:6-8.

The words "image" and "likeness" as they are used in Genesis 1 also seem to indicate that man was capable of growth and development. The image was a reflection or shadow of what it could become. Some day man would share a greater glory. "Likeness" is a word that could be used of a working model of something that will be seen later on a greater scale.

God commanded Adam and Eve to be fruitful and multiply, and fill the earth, and subdue it: and have dominion over the fish of the sea, and over the fowl of the air, and over every living thing that moveth upon the earth.[17] The word "subdue," means to bring under complete control. All the resources of nature were there for man to use. He would have the privilege of discovering them, learning about them, learning how to use them. "Have dominion" can also mean "take dominion." Man did not automatically have dominion over the animal world. Again, he would have to observe, learn, and make use of his intelligence in putting them to their best use.

Hebrews indicates that this subduing and taking dominion over the natural world was, however, only part of God's plan. God wanted man to rule over all His creation, including angels. Man is only temporarily lower than the angels. The angels were created first of all as God's servants to do His will and bidding. But they were also intended to minister or serve "them who shall be heirs of salvation."[18]

Since man has failed, God's purpose has been fulfilled through Jesus. He was made for a little while lower than the angels. He took human nature. In His human nature He was tested just as Adam and Eve

---

[17] Genesis 1:28.   [18] Hebrews 1:14.

were tested. But where they failed, He was obedient. Through His sufferings He shared in our sufferings and won a victory for us over sin. Through His death He won a victory for us over the devil, and set us free from the fear of death.[19]

In this Book Jesus is called the "captain" or leader of our salvation. God's purpose in sending His Son to suffer and die was to lead us back into the sonship and glory we might have had if we had not forfeited it through disobedience.

Looking for a City

Hebrews goes on to connect our hope with the promise given to Abraham. We are to demonstrate diligence, eagerness, zeal with reference to the certainty of our hope to the end. We are not to become slothful or lazy. Instead, we must be followers or imitators "of them who through faith and patience" will inherit the promises at the time of the end.[20] We can afford to do this because God really stands behind His promises.

God not only gave Abraham a promise, He added a solemn pledge in the form of an oath or vow.[21] We have absolute certainty, therefore, that when God makes a promise He will never change His mind. His oath and His promise are two things about which God cannot lie.[22] This gives great encouragement for us who have fled for refuge and found it in Christ. We can lay hold on the hope set before us and find it an anchor of the soul. It is an anchor which will never fail us, because Christ Himself has taken the anchor line with Him into heaven's inner sanctuary and fixed it there in the eternal purpose of God.

---

[19] Hebrews 2:10, 11, 14, 15.
[20] Hebrews 6:11, 12.
[21] Hebrews 6:13, 17.
[22] Hebrews 6:18.

Our hope, then, is for Christ to return, for a resurrection to a better life, a life that made the martyrs willing to die rather than compromise or deny their faith.[23] Then, ultimately, we will obtain a better land than the earthly Canaan, and a better city than the earthly Jerusalem.[24] Because Abraham caught a glimpse of these promises and saw in the distance that city whose builder or architect and maker or creator is God, he embraced or welcomed them. More than that, this hope made him, along with Isaac and Jacob, confess openly that they were strangers or foreigners, aliens and pilgrims or exiles away from home. They desired, they longed for a better country, a heavenly home. Because they focused their hopes and aspirations on God's promise, God was not ashamed to be called (in the Bible) the God of Abraham, Isaac, and Jacob. The implication is, of course, that God is ashamed of anyone who makes earthly things his goal and aim.

Because we can trust God to keep His promise, Hebrews keeps urging us to hold firmly to our faith and hope.[25] We need encouragement in this. First, we must encourage one another. We can do this by stirring up one another to show love and do good. We can do it by being faithful in meeting together in our assemblies.[26] Second, we need also to be patient and courageous, recognizing that the Lord will come, recognizing, too, that anyone who draws back will be lost.[27] We can draw courage from the great crowd of witnesses who are the men and women of faith who have gone before.[28] Third, we can be sure of victory if we keep our eyes fixed on Jesus. He could face

---

[23] Hebrews 9:27, 28; 11:35.
[24] Hebrews 11:13-16.
[25] Hebrews 10:23.

[26] Hebrews 10:24, 25.
[27] Hebrews 10:35-39.
[28] Hebrews 12:1.

the disgrace of the cross without fear because of the joy He saw waiting for Him on the other side of the Resurrection. He is now seated on the right hand of God's throne. By keeping our mind on Jesus and the crown and glory He wants to share with us, we too can face reproach and persecution. We too can refuse to be discouraged or give up.[29]

SHARING CHRIST'S SUFFERINGS

Hebrews saw Christ as King and Priest. Peter in his first epistle emphasizes that we too are to be both kings and priests. This was God's purpose for Israel when He gave them the old covenant at Sinai.[30] They failed, so God opened up the door to both Jews and Gentiles through Christ. We become living stones built into a new spiritual temple, the Church.[31] We also become a holy priesthood, to offer up spiritual sacrifices,[32] acceptable to God by Jesus Christ. Then Peter applies to the Gentiles the very words of God's purpose stated in the old covenant. Though the covenant is new and on a better basis with a better hope, as Hebrews said, God does not change, and His fundamental purposes do not change. God brought Israel out of Egypt to bring them to Himself. He brings us out of the Egypt of sin through Christ to bring us to Himself. So we, too, become a chosen generation (race, nation, people, or family), a people peculiarly God's own (His own in a special way because we are bought with a price, we are twice His), able now to proclaim the praise and miracle-working power of the God who has brought us out of darkness into his marvelous light.[33]

[29] Hebrews 12:1-3; 13:12-16.
[30] Exodus 19:4-6.
[31] 1 Peter 2:5; Ephesians 2:21.
[32] Hebrews 13:15.
[33] 1 Peter 2:9.

Peter's main emphasis in this epistle is, however, the sufferings of Christ which enable us to stand our present tests, trials, and difficulties. Just as it was necessary for Christ to take the cross before the crown, so it is for us.

Because God raised Jesus from the dead we have a new life now and a living hope for the future. God has a rich inheritance reserved or kept in heaven for us where they cannot decay, be defiled, or fade away.[34] Because of this, we can rejoice and be glad, even though for a while now we must be in heavy sorrow or distress brought by the many kinds of temptations, tests, and trials we must now endure. These tests, in fact, are worth the suffering for two reasons. First, they demonstrate that our faith is genuine. Gold, which can perish or be destroyed, is tested by fire. Your faith is worth much more than gold, so it, too, is worth being tested. Second, after we go through the test we will receive praise and honor and glory when Jesus comes again.[35]

God revealed to the Old Testament prophets that the Messiah or Christ would suffer and that glory would follow.[36] This did not happen in their time, but it was written down for our benefit, to encourage us to set our hope on Christ.[37] We must not be surprised, therefore, if we suffer fiery trials. We must not react to them as if they were something strange or unusual. Instead, we should rejoice because we are sharing Christ's sufferings, sufferings that will make us full of joy when Jesus comes.[38]

Peter, like all the other New Testament writers,

[34] 1 Peter 1:3, 4.
[35] 1 Peter 1:7.
[36] 1 Peter 1:11; Isaiah 53.
[37] 1 Peter 1:13.
[38] 1 Peter 4:12, 13.

makes his epistle a call to holiness.[39] Obedience to
this call will bring further occasion to suffer with
and for Christ. Anyone who lives a holy life becomes
a rebuke to worldliness and sin. The result may be
reproach and insults.[40] But we can live this down
if our conversation, or way of living, is so honest
(good, useful, noble, fine) that in spite of their ac-
cusations they will have to recognize our good works
and glorify God in the day of His coming.[41] We
must also arm ourselves with the mind or purpose to
share Christ's sufferings, by identifying ourselves with
His death. To suffer physically, recognizing we are
suffering with and for Christ puts us on the same
side He is on in the battle against sin.[42]

The battle is a real battle. Our adversary the devil
still goes about as a roaring lion seeking someone to
devour. We must be self-controlled and keep on the
watch. We must resist him with a steadfast, firm
faith, recognizing that fellow believers all over the
world are going through the same battles.[43] We must
also be careful not to bring our sufferings on ourselves
by crimes against people or property or by putting
our noses into other people's business.[44] Then, after
we have suffered a while in the will of God, He
will call us to share His eternal glory with Christ
and in union with Him.[45] For when He comes we
will receive a crown of glory that will never fade
or lose its brightness.[46] It will pay us to be patient,
to keep our hopes high, to take the long view. Jesus
is coming soon.[47] We have His promise!

---

[39] 1 Peter 1:14, 15.
[40] 1 Peter 4:14.
[41] 1 Peter 2:12.
[42] 1 Peter 4:1.
[43] 1 Peter 5:8, 9.
[44] 1 Peter 4:15.
[45] 1 Peter 4:19; 5:10.
[46] 1 Peter 5:4.
[47] James 5:8.

QUESTIONS

1. What does our "blessed hope" include?

2. What qualities are necessary if we are to win the race of life? Which one would you say is the most important?

3. What are some of the things that indicate that we were created to reign as kings?

4. What is the guarantee of God's promise and our Christian hope?

5. For what did Abraham look and what does this mean to us?

6. What is Peter's main emphasis in his first epistle?

7. What practical lessons does Peter draw from Christ's suffering and victory?

Books For Further Study

BOYD, FRANK M., *Introduction to Prophecy*. Springfield, Missouri: Gospel Publishing House, 1948.

HORTON, STANLEY M., *Bible Prophecy*. Springfield, Missouri: Gospel Publishing House (Undated Teacher's Manual), 1963.

McCLAIN, ALVA, *The Greatness of the Kingdom*. Grand Rapids: Zondervan Publishing House, 1959.

PEARLMAN, MYER, *Knowing the Doctrines of the Bible*. Springfield, Missouri: Gospel Publishing House, 1958.

PENTECOST, J. DWIGHT, *Things to Come*. Grand Rapids: Zondervan Publishing House, 1958.

RYRIE, C. C., *The Basis of Premillennial Faith*. Neptune, New Jersey: Loizeaux Brothers, 1954.

WALVOORD, JOHN F., *The Return of the Lord*. Grand Rapids: Zondervan Publishing House, 1955.

WILLIAMS, ERNEST S., *Systematic Theology*. (Vol. 3) Springfield, Missouri: Gospel Publishing House, 1953.